J. G Lyall

The Merry Gee-Gee

How to Breed, Break, and Ride Him For'ard Away

J. G Lyall

The Merry Gee-Gee

How to Breed, Break, and Ride Him For'ard Away

ISBN/EAN: 9783337144333

Printed in Europe, USA, Canada, Australia, Japan

Cover: Foto ©Lupo / pixelio.de

More available books at **www.hansebooks.com**

THE MERRY GEE-GEE

How to Breed, Break, and Ride Him
For'ard Away

AND

THE NOBLE ART OF BACKING WINNERS
ON THE TURF

BY

J. G. LYALL

LONDON
F. V. WHITE & CO.
14, BEDFORD STREET, STRAND, W.C.
1899

CONTENTS

CHAPTER		PAGE
I.	How I came to write a Book	1
II.	Breeding	16
III.	Breaking	52
IV.	Riding	81
V.	For'ard away	115
VI.	The Noble Art of backing Winners on the Turf	158

THE MERRY GEE-GEE

THE MERRY GEE-GEE

CHAPTER I

HOW I CAME TO WRITE A BOOK

RETURNING home from Newmarket the other evening after a particularly unsuccessful week, and being in an extra-contemplative mood, the thought recurred to me, as it had so often done before, that I would, by one vehement resolve —a real copper-bottomed, armour-plated, life-and-death resolution — bind myself never to back another horse in a race. Financial matters were about as black as could be with me, and I had taken a week's racing, thinking and hoping to play up a few sovereigns by judicious investment, but it had "come off crabs" (to use a familiar turf vulgarism), as it generally does when one goes as a last extremity and to stop a gap.

Pulling my race-card out of my breast-pocket to review the day's proceedings, I also fished out with it two writs and four county court summonses, all of which demanded immediate attention, so as a preliminary step I carefully tore them into tiny fragments and committed them to the four winds of heaven out of the carriage window; leant back in the corner of the compartment, gazed vacantly at the scudding landscape, and resumed my reverie, with the result that in a few moments I brought down my fist on my knee with unusual gusto, and swore solemnly to myself to have done with backing 'em for as long as I breathed the breath of life. What a career mine had been, too! Surely I ought to write a book, and insert a few experiences—a few of the things I had seen and knew.

"Tickets all ready" at the terminus awoke me from the refreshing slumber into which I had fallen, and, pulling myself together, I remembered my resolve, which was fixed and sealed, and from which nothing in the world should ever turn me. I am impulsive to the last degree, and, candidly, I am not at all sure the old adage as to second thoughts proving the best has proved true on the few occasions in which I have brought it into play. Yes, acting on the impulse of the moment without much consideration is useful sometimes, especially when hounds are running hard, and you successfully negotiate the fence in the corner of the field at which, had you hesitated, your horse would probably have blundered and fallen.

Now, it so happened that on the very next day after my return from Newmarket just recorded, I drove over from Melton Mowbray (where I now reside) to Piper Hole (familiar name to all Leicestershire hunting men) with a young horse in my high brake, and whilst standing there quietly enough he suddenly took fright at some sound or movement, and quick as thought he commenced to kick and plunge as if forty unclean spirits were inside him. He turned the brake over and kicked me as I was falling out, broke both shafts off, tore the harness to smithereens, and made things hum pretty lively for a few minutes. More than that, he has all but smashed my thigh and ribs; consequently, instead of watching the Quorn hounds rattle the cubs round Gartree Hill cover this morning, I am laid in bed sore and envious, and shall probably be here for some little time to come. Thus fate, or what you please to term it, has impelled me to carry out my half-hearted threat of yesterday, viz. to write a book.

It's wonderful how frequently the whole bent of one's life from a given time seems turned by a mere thread, and deviates into what seemed improbable channels ; and certainly, if that beggar hadn't settled me yesterday, I should not at this moment be budding into a real embryo author.

Possibly some of my gentle readers (in all cases made and provided, as the lawyers say)—if there are any such long-suffering individuals born yet—may have had the thought flash through their minds at some period of their existence, "How would it be if I tried to write a book?" Awfully funny sensation when you really ask yourself the question in earnest. "What the deuce shall I write about?" comes the reply. Naturally, the maudlin schoolgirl must write a pathetic love-story. Let me strongly advise her not to start that subject too young, though. I should suggest "Botany" or "Bird Life in the Woods and on the Coast" as a preliminary canter at any age under five and twenty. By then and in the ordinary course she will doubtless have broken four or five men's hearts, or peradventure the man she secretly adores will have gone and married "quite a common-looking creature

—squints, and all sorts of things, don't you know, my dear?" so that by then she will have been "through the mill" sufficiently to take her subject well in hand.

Of course, it is simplicity itself for a bronzed warrior fresh from the Soudan to write of the conquest of the Khalifa, and to scribble by the yard of Dervish valour; but I have chosen for my theme "The Merry Gee-Gee," for is not the love of a horse born in me and grafted in my very nature? As to any claim to a knowledge of my subject, have I not bred many, dealt in them more or less since my school days, broken hundreds, hunted in many countries both fox and stag, owned and trained a few winners and a good many losers, read all the books relating to horses I could ever lay hands on, gone broke, been rough-rider and nagsman, London brakesman and four-in-hand man, driven a hansom, made a book on the course, and gone to bed hungry? This may be only an apprenticeship, may be, and doubtless is, only partially "going through the mill," but it's enough for me, with thanks—very many thanks.

I believe the proper and recognized thing for an out-and-out amateur author such as I am is to engage an editor, or coach, or some such "bird of prey," to knock one's ideas and scribblings into readable shape and sound English, but I will have none of these. I am just going to run riot as my fitful fancy dictates; and if (as is more than probable) none but an old pal or two will ever struggle through it, what matter if it is a disconnected, egotistical, and ungrammatical jumble? One promise I distinctly make, and that is, it shall be candid, even as against myself.

My earliest recollection of anything connected with horses was when, about four years old, I used to ride four or five broomsticks, and kept them all carefully tied up in the nursery, with suitable names for each one.

We worked thirty or forty cart-horses on the farm, and I very soon got to know them all by name, many of which I can remember to this day, although my father died and we left that farm when I was seven years old. That was up on the Lincolnshire Wolds, on the Brocklesby estate of Lord Yarboro', in the good old days when wheat made three, four, and sometimes five pounds a quarter, and wool fifty to seventy shillings per tod. (Present prices: wheat twenty-five shillings, and wool nineteen shillings.)

My old dad was quite the old-fashioned type of farmer—drank a gallon of beer (of his own brewing) per day for fifty-five years, besides liquor, and never had a day's illness in his life. He'd have lived to be a hundred right enough if he hadn't happened an accident. He committed the indiscretion of marrying a second young wife at sixty-five, and in due course became the author of my being, so the beer had not done him so very much harm, had it? He made a rare fuss of me, I can remember, and used to cross-examine me as to which mares the young horses were all out of, etc. We had one hundred and fifty beasts, all red; he wouldn't have one with a white hair on it. There is a Lincolnshire Red Shorthorn Breeders' Association now, and they have an annual sale at Lincoln April Fair.

In those days lots of Lincolnshire farmers hunted in scarlet and drove their broughams—men with fifteen or twenty thousand pounds invested in agriculture; and you would find four or five farmers or their sons in each parish who hunted the little red rover on horses of their own breeding, whilst now you may traverse four or five parishes before you meet with one, and a man on a horse at all is fast becoming a curiosity.

There are no better fellows living than Lincolnshire farmers. Yorkshire and Norfolk farmers are jolly good fellows too. There are right good sorts to be met with here in Leicestershire, and everywhere else, for the matter of that; but I somehow notice a different type of farmer where all grass abounds than where there is a mixed tillage.

Lord Lonsdale, late Master of the Quorn, has been particularly generous and thoughtful to Leicestershire farmers, making all the second horsemen keep together, so that they do as little damage as possible, and also issuing a free register of corn, hay, and straw for sale by farmers all over the Quorn country, and so holding out an inducement to the gentlemen of the hunt to deal with the producer direct.

I hold rather strong opinions, which I am aware are at variance with the generally accepted theory, as to this forage question, viz. that by November well-got new hay is as good as old, and that a very big proportion of what one buys as old oats off the corn-merchant about the same season of the year is either a mixture of new and old or new altogether. Not that I think there is any injurious effect from all this—simply that we are too strongly wedded to a phantom theory, and the victims of a certain amount of imposition into the bargain. Clover hay well got makes a capital change for delicate feeders, and so does sainfoin. Horses that are shy feeders should be coaxed and tempted with what they show a liking for (so long as it is not injurious), and fed often and in small quantities.

A horse has a very small stomach in proportion to cattle and other animals about their own size, hence I favour late stable time for suppering horses in training, and early breakfasts. It is an easy matter for a responsible stableman and the stud-groom to take this matter in turn, and I am convinced of its advantages. Horses at grass are for ever grazing, look at them when one may, and be the pasture ever so luxuriant; and nature sets many examples which science has yet to improve upon.

I am firmly convinced that every horse confined in stables requires salt in some form, and I always give all mine, from cart-horses to race-horses, a lump of rock-salt to lick in their mangers. I am equally certain that nothing like sufficient roots are given horses, especially young ones working and living on corn. Carrots are best for hunters and race-horses, but where these are not available swede-turnips are a good substitute, and equally good for slow work. Mangold wurzel, too, is capital for cart-horses in the spring months, but rather sour up to Christmas.

If a man studies the peculiarities of horses under his charge with intelligent observation, he is sure to find some requiring different methods to others, and a great error is very frequently committed in feeding and treating them irrespective of their different individual peculiarities.

I have had several hunters who would eat enormous suppers and hardly anything before noon. One very good mare I hunted would not eat anything on what she thought was a hunting morning, so I used to "kidd" her by taking her out just a few minutes. That seemed to satisfy her that she had taken her exercise, and she would then eat a feed.

But "Hark back!" This is just what I expected; I am off to hunting matters in the wrong place, and unless I "whip off" I shall kill my fox in cover before the run starts, so here goes for another chapter.

CHAPTER II

BREEDING

I AM going to write very little about the breeding of cart-horses under this heading, as most men who breed them are practical farmers who know quite as much on the subject as I can tell them, but one word I may say in the shape of advice especially applicable to the small occupier who rears an odd foal, and it is a point which I shall emphasize very strongly further on, when we come to hunter-breeding, *i.e.* don't breed from small, under-sized, ill-shaped mares. If any one has a mare of the small and useful class, who may nevertheless have proved a real good slave for the purpose required, he says to himself, "If I sell the old mare she won't make above a fiver, so I'll breed from her, and put her to a Shire horse." If you want to breed a cart-horse, my advice is, let the old mare go for what she will fetch. I'll tell you where to replace her at the same money, and this also applies with equal, or perhaps greater, force to seekers after mares suitable for breeding hunters.

Most of the best cart-horses find their way to London at five years old, and are used up on the stones. They are resold as they gradually show signs of wear, from one job to another, where smartness is less necessary, till they get right off their feet with the cruel hot stones. Their price at the Repository gets down to perhaps seven or eight

C

sovereigns, or even less, but the breeding and great banging frame is still there, and they are not only just as good for breeding purposes, but it is marvellous how many of them recuperate when they get their feet on cool soft ground, even in a few weeks, and many a cart-mare bought in London that can hardly hobble will trot about in a grass field, fairly sound, in a day or two. I have bought some hundreds of low-priced horses in London, so I am not speaking at random.

The Repositories at which intending purchasers will find this class of cart-mare are the Barbican, Elephant and Castle, Edgware Road Repository, and Stapleton's, Commercial Street, East. If you are fastidious as to rubbing shoulders with some terrible dirty scadgers, don't go to Stapleton's, as it adjoins Spitalfields Market, and you meet the veriest dregs of East End costermonger society there. If, on the other hand, your clothes are getting shabby, and you would like to be a veritable toff for the day, go to Stapleton's, and your highest ambition will be gratified. Don't polish yourself up too much, though, or the company will mistake you for a stray duke out for the day, and doing the East End. I have bought some rare cheap horses at Stapleton's for an old song, however, and I commend this course to farmers wanting cheap good mares. Good, sound, weighty cart-horses are likely to continue in good demand at remunerative prices for a long time yet, in spite of motor-cars; but I think the fashionable craze for noblemen breeding shires, and the extravagant prices of a few years ago, is past its zenith.

The runs of fashion in breeding prize

and fancy stock amongst noblemen and millionaires does not change quite as quickly as the fashion in ladies' hats, but it does have fashionable runs and quick changes, and always will so long as there are shoddy millionaires or demi-millionaires knocking about who don't care what they spend so long as they can be in the swim with the cream of society, from the Prince of Wales downwards. The shorthorn craze was on fifteen or twenty years ago, and I remember attending the marvellous sale of Mr. Torr's at Riby, near Grimsby. A heifer that day made 2400 guineas, and others in proportion. To-day really good shorthorns of the best blood make just a few sovereigns more than butchers' or grazing price, and that's all. Every dog has its day, they say, and shorthorns have had theirs. They'll come again, though, in another generation as certain as crinolines, coal-scuttle bonnets, and Dundreary whiskers.

Shropshire sheep were all the rage a few years ago, and Lincoln Longwools took a back seat. To-day Shrops are in the rear, and Lincolns in the van. Only the other day a Lincoln ram of Mr. Dudding's, bred on the same farm as Mr. Torr's heifer above mentioned, was sold for 1000 guineas, and several others at 200 and 300 guineas each.

There were one or two things our forefathers were not such very great duffers at: one was architecture; at least, I don't see any new buildings erected nowadays to lick the old cathedrals. But what concerns us most is the science of breeding; and really, the clever manner in which our ancestors assimilated the breeds of cattle and sheep to the climate and soil of various districts is truly marvellous. Take Shropshire or Suffolk sheep to winter on turnips in Lincolnshire, and they will do no good whatever. Take Lincolns to Warwickshire or Staffordshire, and they will quickly lose the staple and lustre of their wool. Breed them there two or three seasons, and you will hardly tell them from shortwools: they lose their characteristics. You must not take Welsh Runts or Hereford cattle further northeast than Leicestershire, or the stronger grass and sharp air will settle their pretensions; they must give place to the hardier shorthorn, and so on.

How many times does one hear the argument advanced that you seldom get chops and steaks in the provinces equal to those in town?—an opinion in which I entirely concur, so far as regards the best hotels and restaurants. Permit me to explain the reason. The London highclass butcher knows the particular county or district which produces the best-quality meat at given periods of the year. Let us follow the seasons with beef, for example, and start at Christmas. Top quality then is Scotch and Norfolks, because the roots, pulse, and fodder in those localities are the finest grained and best, hence the meat the same. Norfolks will keep on to, say, the second week in June, long after the Scots are exhausted, and will then be superseded by the first crop of early grass-fed shorthorns off the Lincolnshire fens and marshes. Just before August Herefords assume the command, followed, seven or eight weeks later, by Runts. If (for example) you took a Hereford and Runt of equal weight to Islington the first week in August, and asked a high-class butcher £20 each for them, he would say,

If you like to separate them I'll give you £21 for the Hereford; but the Runt is no use to me, it is not in season yet. Take the same two beasts on October 1, and he will exactly reverse his tale. He knows that which his provincial *confrère* is ignorant of, and has not the facility to ascertain.

I have had a very large and successful practice as an auctioneer, and have sold in the Metropolitan Market. For some years, I dare say, I sold more sheep than any man in England—some 200,000 per annum—but I've lost more in a day racing than I made in a year selling, or I should not be writing this " tract." Many a time I have sold in Islington Cattle Market at 7 a.m., taken Hinckley Market in Warwickshire from one to three, and had a four hours' spell selling unredeemed pledges in our mart at Leicester from six to ten—all on a Monday, and just a tidy day's work.

We will now proceed to discuss the breeding of blood-stock; and granting, for argument's sake, that you are wealthy and entirely independent of all monetary considerations, you can afford to keep mares in your harem with twisted legs, cow-hocks, contracted feet, or roarers, and mate them with stallions at 300 or 400 guinea fees, because so long as you can produce a flying two-year-old (which by some merciful dispensation of Providence may perchance train on into a three-year-old) that will carry your colours first past the post a few times at Epsom, Ascot, or Goodwood, your wish will be gratified, the goal reached, as the fickle goddess dictates; but please do not, "my millionaire," tell the country you are doing this thing for your country's good and to improve the breed of horses. Luck has a loud voice in breeding blood-stock (as well as in other pursuits), and will have, in spite of all figure systems, which, as applied to producing race-horses, doubtless has its merit, inasmuch as it favours breeding from lines of winners or lines which have produced winners. I believe in breeding from winners, and they win in nearly all shapes; but if you keep on persistently breeding for a few generations from winning mares with weak loins or sickle-shaped hocks, you will very soon perpetuate a breed with backs so narrow that they will cut the man in half who bestrides them, and with hind legs at right angles at the hocks.

But, after all, what consequence is this to the *parvenue*, so long as he owns winners, with the accompanying *kudos*, independent of all gambling interests? There are exceptions, of course, and I should say about one breeder in a thousand breeds for his country's good. That's not many, is it? and it won't take many fingers to count them. If, as a middle-class man of moderate means, you have an inclination to breed a few thoroughbreds either for sale as yearlings or to race yourself, buy a few mares, as your accommodation or means allow—winners preferred, free from malformation or hereditary disease, big and roomy, any whole colour except greys or roans, mind they stand square on their legs, and walk and trot square in their action to you and from you—and put them to a stallion of a similar stamp at a moderate fee, and you will very likely breed a race-horse; but if at two years old your colt is too slow for flat-racing, you can lay it by for steeple-chasing or hunting, or as a stallion for the home or foreign market. You will always find a sale for your horse if he comes anything like true to his parentage, and will not have to part with him for a tenner.

Perhaps one reason why I emphasize the desirability of them standing and moving true is because I at one time held a commission to buy stallions for a foreign government to sire troopers, and I know how exceedingly difficult suitable horses are to find. A Leicestershire hunter may be forgiven for having to wear boots on his fetlocks or pasterns if he belongs to a man with a big stud, and can carry his owner in front of 400 tearing and envious followers for forty minutes from Ranksboro' Gorse or Billesdon Coplow one day a week or once in ten days; but put a heavy dragoon with his baggage on the same gee, and let him undertake a protracted march under a tropical sun over rugged ground — bad shoeing, and his leather boots worn through—and the said gee will be resting his bruised fetlocks, and the said dragoon cursing the government that sent him a bent-legged brute like this to ride. Experience and observation rather force me to the belief that not only in breeding horses, but also in breeding animals of all kinds, it is better to have full size in the sire, whilst a trifle under-size is permissible in the dam.

Without entering at length into the saturation theory, which avows with some evidence of truth that the influence of a given sire on his progeny from a given dam, is partially transmitted to the second progeny of the same mare by a fresh sire, but which theory is too intricate for discussion here, I am nevertheless pretty certain that colour of skin and feather comes more from the sire, whilst make and shape is handed down from the dam. For instance, if you mate a Berkshire boar with a pure white sow you will get more black spots on the litter of young than by mating a white boar with a Berkshire sow. In choosing a stallion for your mare, besides making certain that he counteracts in his formation any deficiency in your mare, take care the strain of blood, as proved by results in producing winners, nicks in properly, and also, if possible (and especially if breeding for sale), that the stallion has sired some winners already, or is in a large stud where he will have ample facilities given him to make a name for himself, as it will give immense impetus to the sale of your yearling if some winners by the same sire are "getting home," and shedding lustre on his fame.

The "Special Commissioner" who writes in the *Sportsman* is the best-versed public man in breeding theories, and he generously gives most courteous and gratuitous advice to blood-stock breeders in the columns of that journal, as to what lines of blood will mate advantageously with their mares. Manage as one will, however, and lavish what money you please, there is no commanding success in the breeding of blood-stock. The late Lord Falmouth could breed classic winners just like ordinary mortals shelling peas. The Rothschilds, for some time previous to these last few seasons, struck an unlucky vein, with Sir Bevys alone to break the monotony. Very unlucky, too, was Lord Roseberry for long enough up to the Ladas, Sir Visto, and Velasquez era. The Duke of Westminster had a wonderful run a few seasons ago, which has received, let us hope, only a temporary check; whilst the Duke of Portland, who a while back could breed nothing but Derby winners, can now hardly win a selling race. When Hermits were carrying all before them, the Blankney yearlings used to fetch enormous averages, but now, although they have Galopin and Friars Balsam to perpetuate fame, their yearling average for several seasons has been a sorry contrast to fifteen years ago. Sir J. Blundell Maple, who has an enormous stud with perfect clockwork arrangements at Chilwickbury, gets only a miserable return in the number of winners it yields.

Luck and fashion runs in grooves and

cycles, and it is not in the power of mortal man to command success where the element of chance comes in. Some men apparently cannot do wrong for years in anything they undertake, and they are apt to arrogate to themselves every turn in fortune's wheel as the outcome of their own cleverness. When disaster ultimately overtakes such as these (as it usually does, sooner or later), they generally howl like whimpering curs.

The luckiest small breeder I wot of is my friend John C. Hill, of Willoughton, who was a neighbouring farmer of mine at one time. He generally kept a hunt-chaser years ago that could win a race at the local meetings, and rode himself. An extraordinary good man to hounds he was, especially on certain days. He is a man of few words, but when you saw him craning his neck at the coverside of a morning, and his hat jammed well in his neck, you needn't ask any questions. Jack meant going, and without bucketing his horse at first, he was certain to be there if they ran for two hours. One day he bought Moorhen, by Hermit, a good-looking, sizey mare, for, I think, 250 guineas. This was in the days when hunt-chasers had to be qualified by M.F.H. certificates, and not by being placed in a steeplechase, as now; and Moorhen won many races, sometimes "owner up," but more generally piloted by Mr. Brockton, without flying at very high game, but still winning occasionally small open hurdle races and steeplechases. He was bid £1500 for Moorhen, but wouldn't sell, although it hardly looked a "turning away" price for a tenant farmer, but it was all for the best, as she presently bred

Gallinule, sire of Wildfowler, this year's St. Leger winner; Pioneer, third in the Derby; and another yearling which he sold for £2500 to Colonel North, so altogether she must have put something not far short of £10,000 into her owner's pocket, and he was offered £4000 for her as a brood mare.

This happens to be the day after the Duke of York Stakes at Kempton Park, and I notice the three placed horses are all by Gallinule, as well as the winner of the next race, quite a unique incident, and there really seems no end to old Moorhen's influence on the fortunes of mankind. There are many examples of this in turf history, notably Blink Bonny, the founder of the fortunes of the I'Anson family. One good horse in judicious hands is the foundation-stone of a middle-class fortune, gambling apart.

I am not going to say many words about the breeding of the present-day prize hackney, as for the generality of them I have the profoundest contempt. Three-parts of the bad-shouldered hackneys one sees at shows, with their tiring, climbing action, would drop down dead if driven five and twenty miles alongside a sharp blood-horse on a country road. They make a decent flash driven the length of Hyde Park, but beat themselves if they go much further. My model of a hackney is Mr. Carnley's Norbury Squire, who has won more prizes than any other horse in England in harness and hack classes at the shows this past few seasons, I should say. At any rate, I have seen him beat all the other recognized champions in turn; and whilst it goes without saying that he has extraordinary fine all-round action, with lots of fire and courage, what charms me is his lovely shoulder, and the knowledge that, although by a hackney stallion, he is actually out of a mare by Hermit! I must have blood—thoroughbred blood, closely allied one side or the other; and it is in this respect the so-called hackney is deficient and a disappointment in nineteen cases out of twenty.

Nowadays, when everybody rides bikes, the ordinary ride-and-drive horse there was always a certain trade for years ago has become a drug in the market and profitless to breed. Polo ponies have their own registered Polo Stud-book, and beyond expressing an opinion that if you breed long without a pure, small thoroughbred or Arab sire you will soon get wide of the mark, I will dismiss them. A covert hack proper I look upon as an enlarged polo pony or miniature thoroughbred, and, besides being a good walker, must be able to do a sling gallop seven or eight miles without drawing rein, losing his courage, or displaying much outward and visible sign of fatigue; and obviously one must not wander far from the thoroughbred to produce this class of goods.

Carriage-horses are very valuable and very saleable goods when big enough and well matched in colour and contour. Hardly any game pays better in the dealing line than the match-carriage-horse trade. I was breaksman for one of the leading London dealers one season when I had gone broke racing—did nothing but drive pairs and four-in-hands from morning to night. It's a very nice art putting raw ones together, making them step and go together, carry their heads level, and giving them manners. They take no end of matching, and you have to scour the country fairs to attain your end. You have hardly any chance to match unless you have a big stable and a good connection. You may go to country fairs and buy, say, seven horses at different times, any one of which you think will match the other, but when you get home you will be lucky if you can couple two pairs out of the seven to fit a connoisseur. But you are assured of a big profit when you can match. You buy a green four-year-old at a fair for £80, and a good price too, perhaps, for him individually as he stands. You do ditto at another fair—that is £160 for the two. Take them home and find they match, give them nice manners, and they are worth £400 or £500. Then they are not the same expense and risk in schooling and getting fit that hunters are, nor do they require such expensive living to get in condition. They simply want jogging about in a double brake in traffic with knee-caps and boots all round for an hour or so per day.

These reflections and observations lead me to lay stress on the fact that you cannot do without the middle-man, or dealer, in any trade. The nobleman wants to go and select his pair of carriage-horses where he can have some choice, and they are ready to hand. Besides, I'll defy any one to account to a nicety for people's taste in horseflesh. I know of my own knowledge (lawyer-like term again) that you may invite a customer, whose requirements you think you know, to come and look at a certain horse you think will suit exactly, and ten to one he will say, "Ah well, no, I don't think he is quite what I'm looking for;" and he will stroll round, and eventually buy the bay out of the corner box of the back stable that you would never have dreamt of showing him.

No; the world requires the middleman in the horse trade, the cattle trade, and all other trades that I am at all conversant with. Besides, if by the wave of a mystic wand, dealers, auctioneers, and other middle-men could have their present means of obtaining a livelihood extinguished, they would exist by some other means, I presume. The food they eat and the clothes they wear would not become so much spoil for the rest of the community.

I have given hackneys short shrift up to now in this chapter, but will give them this chance—that if you have a big thoroughbred mare or hunting mare, providing they are of good whole colour, of nice symmetry, and standing and going square with moderately good action, you may put such to a good big hackney sire in the hope of breeding carriage-horses. The other cross is to mate a big thoroughbred sire of suitable colour and without twisted legs to a big hackney mare. Remember a carriage-horse should be built on lengthy, flowing lines of graceful symmetry, not short, coupled, or goose-rumped. Avoid white legs, and by selecting a stallion that will in all probability be available another season or two you may possibly breed a match pair, but this is by no means a certainty.

Coming now to the breeding of hunters, it may almost be laid down as a *sine quâ non* that the sire should be thoroughbred, but one does very occasionally come across a crossbred sire which would get hunters from thoroughbred mares, but it is most exceptional.

Some years ago I did tumble across a rare good stallion of this description who proved himself a real good hunter sire. He was by a thoroughbred horse out of a so-called hackney mare showing lots of quality, but which was in the H.S.B., and as a matter of fact I bought a foal out of this mare by a thoroughbred horse with which I won several steeplechases. I bought this stallion for the Indian Government as an experiment, and he was most successful out there getting troopers. For breeding hunters I should myself never have put this horse to any but clean thoroughbred mares.

To go back to the safest and most

popular cross, *i.e.* thoroughbred sire on a three-quarter-bred mare, let us for a moment discuss the thoroughbred sire. I must again, at the risk of repetition, draw attention to the essential for square standing and true action. If your sire dishes, or is cow-hocked and goes wide behind, his progeny is pretty sure to do the same. If you have a habit of wearing your own boots unlevel or are knock-kneed, your children will be pretty certain to have the same tendency in a reduced degree. You have only to look at the soles of your own boots and your children's for proof of this argument.

The various masters of hounds in a great many counties generally offer the services of good sires to the farmers and puppy walkers, as also do many of the large landowners, notably the Duke of

Portland. Partly from this source and partly because the Horse Improvement Commissioners some years ago took the Royal grant off the Queen's Plates and gave the money for premium stallions, the country is now quite inundated with good sires.

I hold the opinion myself, private enterprise would for several years, at least, provide sufficient suitable stallions, and that the present Imperial grant flows in a wrong channel. It is the mares that are not to be found. It is a sweeping assertion to make, but I do not believe there are more than forty or fifty mares in farmers' hands in Leicestershire and Rutland at all fit to be classed as hunter brood mares. There are, however, hundreds of under-sized, angular, three-cornered, nondescript mares bred from with miserable results, and I think that if the Horse Commission turned their attention wholly or partly to the registration of and the granting of premiums to mares, more beneficial results would accrue.

I am quite certain, if a farmer will attend Aldridge's or the other London Repositories I have named, he can with patience buy some really grand samples of hunter brood mares for ten guineas each, or perhaps less. This is where the good mares meet their last market. I have seen some grand ones included in drafts from Messrs. Tilling of Peckham, who are the largest private job-masters in England. When their wheelers get off their feet on the stones, and can scarcely hobble, they send them to the Repositories to be sold for what they will fetch; but a few weeks on the cool ground alters all that, though they would hobble again if they returned to the stones. Breed hunters big, and up to weight if you can; these are what command the money. I have known several light, cleanly, active mares that have taken their place in Lincolnshire farm teams, themselves only two or three removes from a thoroughbred sire, who, when mated to a blood horse have shown a marvellous capability for breeding weight-carrying hunters, and have proved a small fortune to their owners. In such as these it is, of all things, absolutely necessary that their shoulders should be well placed.

The Hunter's Improvement Society is a well-meaning institution, but I am not sanguine of their efforts being crowned with any great measure of success. Private enterprise will always meet such requirements as carry their own reward. The price the Government pays for troopers is quite inadequate remuneration to the producer, neither is the current price of any middle-class nondescript horse, be he sound as a bell and quiet as a lamb. It is only the best and truest specimens of each individual class of horse that are any source of profit to the farmer who breeds and rears them, consequently the man who breeds from unsuitable mares or mates good ones badly is blind to his own interests, and is courting disappointment and loss.

There are thousands of acres of moderate land in this country, the rent of which is now reduced to almost a nominal sum, and whilst such land is in many cases entirely unfitted to the grazing of cattle and sheep, much of it will do horses well; and I firmly believe that by buying mares at low prices, thus reducing the risk to a minimum, and by suitably mating them, there is remuneration in store for such enterprise. How much better business it would be for farmers to breed something at small expense such as I have suggested, with the possibility of making from £70 to £100 at four years old, than purchasing the three-cornered wretches they are for ever buying out of the second-class Irish and Welsh droves at fairs and markets! These really are the dearest class of horse a man can possibly buy, as with the best of luck they never can, at any subsequent period of their career, ever be worth more than their original cost out of the drove.

I have not any statistics at hand giving the number of horses imported annually from America to this country;

but I know it to be something enormous the last few years, and this gives much cause for reflection.

It is only just for a few weeks in mid-winter these brood mares require a little cheap corn just to warm and hold them together, and by allowing the foals to remain with their mothers as long as there is any natural support, much expense need not be expended on them. Of course, I am not alluding to young race-horses, which must be forced to early maturity to the utmost. Thoroughbred yearlings intended for sale are often ruined by the artificial means used to force them. Their bodies get too heavy for their immature legs and joints, and their feet get hot, thus fostering disease. Whilst breeders and trainers all know the evil results of this system, the fact remains that if you take a yearling to

Doncaster or Newmarket sales, looking rough and backward, and cutting a bad figure alongside his neighbours, you can't sell him.

CHAPTER III

BREAKING

BLESS me, I am over another fence, and picking out a place in the next! Only fancy having written two chapters, and starting another! A hundred times I have been on the verge of tearing up the whole lot, and having no more of this terrible job. I have counted the words on the lines, and the lines on the pages, and calculated how many will fill a book. I remember indulging in this sort of thing over my first essay at school, and I suppose it is so with every one who writes a first book. My people have to speak over and over again to me before attracting my attention from staring into vacant space, and my hair is loosening at the roots. I shall be perfectly bald-headed before this *magnum opus* is finished. I am wondering how authors come to be depicted the long-haired wretches they generally are. It's a puzzler they should have any thatch at all. What bothers me a lot is any sort of division into chapters, and I begin to think I must either call in aid or collapse. No matter; I promised my readers (if any) a jumble, and a jumble it shall be.

Even as some men are born to command, to make great generals, schoolmasters, brigands, pirate chiefs—what you will—so are some men born with an indescribable natural control over the lower animals. Dogs follow such men in a few hours, horses bend to their will, pigeons settle on their shoulders, and elephants dance jigs to their bidding. Patience, firmness, and an equable temperament are the primary essentials of such. I have known Galvayne, and hosts of such trainers, and had innumerable drinks, cigars, and pleasant conversations with no end of circus high-school masters, and also have the pleasure of knowing Captain and Mrs. Hayes, who have written some estimable and instructive books, and been touring in "furrin' parts," giving interesting examples of their proficiency on wild and unmanageable horses, which quickly come under their control and carry Mrs. Hayes contentedly round the arena. As my boy Frank and I break from fifty to a hundred a year without assistance, and are seldom more than three days before we ride and drive them, our experience will do for ordinary purposes; and when one writes a book, it is, after all, perhaps as well to put something in it which may be of use to the common or garden mortal.

I may as well introduce Frank before we go further, as he may crop up again. He is not yet fifteen, and I think I brought him out the youngest horseman on record. He rode his first pony-race when he was eight, at Kyme, in Lincolnshire. After that I soon apprenticed him to myself, and he had his first mount on the flat on Eheu at Doncaster, when Throstle won the St. Leger, before he was eleven. He rode his first steeplechase last autumn at Leicester, when he was fourteen, and made all the running for two and a half miles against eleven runners and Ford of Fyne, who won. He rode five steeple-chases last spring, and this summer he has ridden in ninety-three jumping competitions all over England, winning nineteen firsts, and being forty-seven times in the first three. I hope to see him win a grand National some day. He ought to be flat-race riding now, but I have no horses running at the present time, and other trainers have their own boys bringing out, and would not put up an outside boy (who has not had the opportunity to bring himself to the front) for worlds.

A good apprentice is often the "best horse in the stable" to a trainer, but he must be bound to them; and if you send a young boy out, and he looks like getting beefy, they will never bother about him. He sinks into oblivion; learns such riding as he can pick up from riding in the string; learns to hold on by the reins, which he ought not to do; gets bullied if he is nervous or retiring, and a crack on the head if he is a bit cocky.

All horses should be haltered and taught to lead when they are foals, whilst they are weak and hardly any trouble, for they never forget it. When I was farming 1000 acres up in Lincolnshire and bred a lot of foals, I used to amuse myself during a frost partly by driving the hunters tandem and partly by teaching the foals to lead. They are not very strong, and easily mastered, and have not the strength to damage themselves as older ones have.

In starting an untouched two or three year old, first drive him into a box, and go in to him with a strong halter and a stick, closing the door to prevent his attention being called to extraneous objects. Speak low soothing words to him or whistle—it answers the same purpose. He will snort and his eyes flash fire, but it is from fear; he knows no vice as yet—that he may acquire later on through wrong usage, but not without. Touch him lightly with the stick on his shoulders or quarters. Rub him with the stick all over by degrees till he takes no notice of it; he may kick at it once or twice, but take no notice, he will soon leave off. With your stick on his quarters, extend your hand to his neck or shoulders, and if he shrinks back, give light taps on his quarters with the stick to bring him to his original standing place. He will soon let you rub him with your hand and the end of the halter as freely as with the stick.

Perspiration will now be dropping off him, and tears running from his eyes. Admit your assistant to tap his quarters, whilst you put on the halter as quietly as possible, followed by a leather headstall, and then adjust the bit so as to barely touch the corners of his mouth. Up to now you have not ceased whistling, and, on the principle of earliest impressions being the most lasting, you will find whistling have a soothing effect on him for a long time to come. Take the halter in one hand and the stick in the other, and accompanying a tap on the quarters say the familiar "Coop," and slightly pull the halter. If he throws his head about, don't pull against him: ten men can't hold him yet. He will, however, soon advance to the other end of the box. "Good boy. Coop" again, and so on. The voice has a most powerful and magical effect on the horse, and you should always use the same word to indicate your desires; but of that more anon.

After adjusting knee-caps, and a strong rope to the headstall, a difficulty will present itself getting him to the titting-post, or tree. You must select a place with soft surroundings, or he will damage himself. I used to have a post in the middle of a straw yard on purpose. Possibly he will lead quietly beside an old mare to the post, to which fasten the end of the long halter. Now the fun begins, and he will have a rare go at that post; but as soon as he finds himself beaten, a child can hold him. Lead him round each way, and put on the rest of the breaking-tackle. Then lead him back to his box, and tie him up for two or three hours. Better let him stop tied a few days, except when you want him to champ his bits and walk about the box, as it will be easier at this stage to break him to standing tied. Mind your rope is strong. A horse should never know his own power over man: once he gains that knowledge it takes a lot to deceive him again.

Last year I broke a big strong four-year-old three-quarter-bred cart-horse. He was strong as an elephant and wild as a hyena. He was a lively joker this. With one exception, no human being had ever been within twenty yards of him—been running wild on Burrough Hills all his life. He managed to break the first rope, and after that broke every rope in Burrough village, I verily believe. In a few days I drove his owner about the stalls in Melton Market with him, and let a little boy of mine, ten years old, ride him.

Don't leave the tackle on your horse more than about three hours at a stretch, and if he does not work his bit, change it for another and hang it rather loose in his mouth. Loosen the side-reins when you want to lead him, putting your right hand on his back and giving him the necessary taps on his off quarter. Put on a fast or standing martingale adjusted to the bit before you put on the long reins, and practise him to these first in the box, and teach him to act to the voice and the motion of your hand and whip, as his mouth is young yet, and sensitive to the slightest pressure. Bearing in mind that he is impressionable of all things, particularly to the voice, always speak clear and distinct, saying simply, "Coop," "Whoa," "Stand over," or "Come here," as the case may be, accompanying your request by a gentle tap or draw of the rein. It is better for one man only to work the colt at these early stages, till he knows a bit, as it is highly essential to say to him only the right thing in the right place. For example, you require him to stand over, and you repeat these words and no other, accompanied by a tap, till in a very few moments he will have learned his lesson and comply with eagerness; but if, after the lapse of half an hour, a stranger comes and, requiring him to "stand over," says, "Now then," or "Get up," or "Hello," or "Come here," is he not speaking in a foreign language to him, and undoing what you have taught? Teach him the alphabet of "coop" and "whoa," and you can drive him about the streets with impunity. Run him round always as much one way as the other, or his mouth will be getting one-sided.

You can lift a light boy across his back in the box, now first one side, then the other, and put him up and lead the colt round with the boy on, and in a few minutes he will ride him all right in the box—that is, if the boy knows how to speak to him and enforce his requests. I am not in favour of dumb jockeys, and never hardly use them. They may be of some use on a dead-mouthed older horse, but then their effect is only temporary, and they may be permissible on a colt who is difficult to make champ the bit, but not for long.

A colt should be taught, by the use of fixed side-reins, that "so far and no further shalt thou go" is a golden maxim for him to follow, and the yielding to pressure of the elastic reins of the dumb jockey tends to imbue him with the notion that he has only to pull hard enough to gain a certain mastery. Generally the same day as we first ride our colts we line them in harness a few minutes, and then put them in the brake; they are so subservient to your bidding and taken aback by this new obedience, that they are less trouble then than after a few days' consideration. As you put your colt in, be careful to rub him well with a short stick wherever a fresh strap or the shafts are likely to touch, so as to take the nervousness off, and again whistle to him. Loosen your standing martingale a little, so that he can reach to the collar easily; and run an extra pair of reins through the bit and fasten to the turret of the harness-pad, by which you will have great control in case of emergency. Rattle the trap about and fuss and coax him a bit, and with a "Coop" he'll walk off right enough. I put a lot of hunters in harness here in the spring for the hunting people, and seldom spend more than ten minutes over them before putting them in and driving them.

For kickers, take a plough-line or cord about as thick as an ordinary clothes-line; make a small noose, and put the cord through the horse's mouth with the noose close up. Take the cord over his head behind his ears, threading the head-stall—and, bringing it down, run it through the noose and back upwards through the bearing-rein ring of the throatlash, holding the end of the cord, and as soon as he is in the act of kicking give the cord a jolly sharp jerk, and it will fetch his head up quick and give him a rare twitch; rate him well with a sort of *yarrh!* and after a few doses of this his head will go up with the yarrh! without even pulling the cord. A ring at the end of the cord is preferable to a cord noose, in that you can relax the punishment quicker, as you should the instant he is a good boy. Punish your horse quickly for wrong-doing, and as quickly relax when the desired end is attained.

I have a rearing-bit for rearers, which, with a fast martingale attached, presses the top jaw uncomfortably, and answers with some horses; but the best cure I know for rearing in riding-horses is to shove them in harness, and when they rear punish them with a severe whip inside the thigh, which is the most vulnerable part of a horse. The secret of exacting your wishes from a horse is to cause, by whip, spur, or rein, the fact of wrong-doing to become uncomfortable or unbearable to him; but the moment he bends to your desire the pain must cease, or he will never distinguish right from wrong. Elephants are the easiest animals to train, and them and dogs you can punish for wrong-doing a certain period after the offence, and they will understand what it is for, but not so a horse. It must be conveyed to the latter animal in touch with the action. You can whip your setter for running in to fur, or your foxhound for riot, on his return to the guns or the pack, and he knows what it's for; but if you whip your horse for hitting his timber, it will only cause him to rush at the next lot of rails and go through them pell-mell. You must fasten some timber, and line him over so that if he hits it he will fall, and he will take care of himself next time.

If a horse (an old hunter, for instance) is a fair demon taking to his harness, there is no more effectual remedy than yoking him to a set of chain-harrows in a big grass field with long gears. He can kick and plunge to his heart's content till he tires; he will hurt neither himself nor you, and it settles him splendidly. I made a good boy of that grey from Burrough at this game before I put him in my brake. Give them one or two doses per day as the disease varies. Mind their shoulders, though; nothing creates nappiness so quickly as asking them to face pinched shoulders. If young horses seem naturally averse to facing a collar (or are collar-proud, as it is termed), it is a good plan to line them well in harness, with the collar fastened tight to the breech-band, and a pair of imaginary shafts in the shape of two poles tied to his sides.

The American half-bred mustangs they brought over in considerable quantities a few years ago were most antagonistic to harness. I broke several out of a lot I bought, and although I could drive them myself, it took very little to upset them, and they were never very reliable. They were demons to strike you at first. I used to cure them by fastening two legs together, and by galvayning them. They were very hardy beasts, and I had two fairly good hunters out of the lot.

Young horses always seem to go better in a town than in the country at first; there are so many strange sights in a town to attract them, they seem lost in wonderment, whilst in a country lane they magnify the slightest unusual sight into an apparition. I used to drive fat fresh four-year olds in the brake along the Old Kent Road apparently unmindful of anything, and the same horses would have had fits at sight of a barrel-organ in a country lane. The side streets of a town are capital for teaching them to turn the shafts, they naturally follow the bend of the road. Nothing like a good double brake for bringing a raw recruit to his bearings. Since getting my spill the other day, I am more than ever an advocate for a long-shafted low brake, something like a milk float, as against the high brake, as the sensation when they hook it with you in these is the reverse of pleasant, and you are " so long coming to the ground!" when you get turned over.

After your young horse has got through his infant school days—*i.e.* just quiet to ride and drive—a higher system of education must commence, as really good manners go such a very long way towards successful sale.

Assuming, for argument's sake, you have a high-class harness-horse, he will now have to endure the martyrdom of a big curb-harness bit, because they are in vogue, and he must be fashionable, or he will be nowhere; he must be taught to stretch out when he stands, and put all the life and courage possible into his action when in motion without breaking. If he throws his head up, he must wear a martingale to his nose-band, and he must wear a bearing-rein. I am not an advocate for bearing-reins for country wear, especially where hilly, but in town it looks very bad form to see a horse raking his head to the ground, and standing too much at ease whilst his owner stops to address a friend, or is shopping; and you can hardly keep a young fiery horse whipped up to his bearings without confusion. I believe the foreigners excel us in the pains they bestow in giving manners to their carriage-horses; and one sees some splendidly appointed turn-outs in the Champs Elysées, for instance.

Now, if our youngster of three weeks' or a month's tuition is to graduate for a hunter, he must be taught the use of a double-reined bridle, to open gates, stand the crack of a whip, walk away from other horses, and do all manner of things before he will pass muster as an educated gentleman. During all this period, let him still stick to the fast martingale adjusted to the rings of the bridoon. I am a very great believer in the efficacy of the martingale. It causes the bit to play on the bars of the mouth instead of getting right up into their jaws in their breaking days, and keeps them under control later on. Captain Hayes is a great believer, too, in fast martingales; he, however, goes rather further than I, and would hunt in them, and has in his book snap-shot illustrations of horses jumping fences in them, to prove they do not interfere with them when properly adjusted. I grant all this when jumping only an ordinary fence, but nevertheless there are times in crossing a country—when, for example, your horse has plunged into an unjumpable drain, got partially bogged, and a steep bank the other side—when they certainly could not stretch their necks and heads the requisite length if the martingale was sufficiently tight to be of use in other respects. I would never put a curb on a young horse with hounds till he knows his business fairly well. Two snaffles and a running martingale are best for some time; a curb only irritates him: let him get used to that in his slow work at home.

I have had many arguments with

practical men as to whether the running martingale should be on the curb or snaffle reins. Lord Lonsdale, late Master of the Quorn, had nearly all his horses—huntsman, whips, and his own—ridden in martingales on the curb-rein. Doubtless, if a horse throws his head or star-gazes when nearing his fence, the check of the martingale is far more acute upon the curb-rein than the snaffle, and a horse will combat the resistance with greater determination on the snaffle. Still, on the other hand, if your horse shows temper, and rears, and is nappy at leaving the crowd, you are far more likely to pull him over end with the martingale on the curb, as it is the martingale-rein on which you depend in such case. So there are arguments for and against, and it is better to keep an open mind than wax too dogmatic; but it is beyond question that men should study more fully the adaptation of bridles to horses' mouths than trying to force the mouth to any bridle. Many older horses that have a season or two's hunting experience in them, but who, for all that, are of a hot and impetuous disposition, answer better in two snaffles than a curb. The one makes a dead pull, while the other you can draw through his mouth a little, and thus stop him. I have known horses that hardly could be held in a curb-bridle, let it be of the Mohawk pattern or what it might; and there is a horse Frank rode jumping a few times this summer who has had the bone of his jaw fractured with a big curb and long lever, and they say no man can hold him in a curb, yet this boy holds him comfortably in a crank snaffle and a martingale.

The initiatory jumping-lessons given

the young hunter should be on the long rein, and you want some assistance unless you have properly made schooling fences, as he must on no account be allowed to know that there is any possibility whatever of refusing. One successful wrong step takes no end of counteracting, and once a young horse of wilful disposition gets a knowledge of refusing, it takes a capable and determined horseman to cure him.

After putting knee-caps and bandages on your horse, lunge him over a fixed bar, putting it quite low and taking care not to sicken him by going over too often. Serve him the same over an open ditch, and either a gorse fence or small hedge. You will soon see whether he is what is called a natural jumper, going freely, jumping big, and seeming to enjoy himself, or whether he is clumsy at the game, nervous, and showing a decided reluctance. In the former case you may ride him alone over the jumps, teaching him to turn and go over where you want him; but in the latter case you will do well to have some one to give you a lead, to lend enchantment and give him confidence. Out hunting at first, too, he may follow a lead for a while, but not too long, or he will soon be wanting to tear after every horse he sees jump a fence. Ride him round and round in circles, too, first one way and then the other, when the crowd are standing about at cover corners—it teaches him to go exactly where you want him instead of hanging on to other horses; and be sure and mind he doesn't kick any one or any of the hounds that may come bounding out of the fence close to his heels.

Whilst some people seem to have the happy knack of doing the right thing in the right place with horses, others always do that which they ought not to do. If I take a horse home which we have been breaking, and say, "Now, Mr. So-and-so, we've brought your horse back, and he goes right enough, but he's got a particularly light mouth, which is sure to harden plenty in time. Let's put him in your trap, and you can drive him and see how he goes." We put him in, and he takes the reins, and in spite of what I've said as to his mouth, instead of speaking to him or clicking in the usual way, he gives him a good old-fashioned agricultural job in the mouth with the reins to start with, which either makes him rear or run back, and no wonder. Or—illustration No. 2—if I say, "Mr. So-and-so, I've had some bother with the mare; she's been a bit light behind, but is all right now, so just play the whip lightly on her neck or withers when she requires it, till she gets warm to her work." Dear old So-and-so, forgetting or careless of all instructions, and from long usage with t'owd mare in the stable, gives her a friendly prod with his ash plant just close to the roots of her tail. Then the band plays.

CHAPTER IV

RIDING

IF it were not for hunting and racing, it is fair to presume that, since the immortal bike has come to hold supreme sway, riding on horseback would become obsolete—shown in circuses, perhaps, and looked on as an old-world curiosity and an example of semi-barbarous days in picture-galleries a century or two hence, and nothing more; but, thank Heaven! bikes can't jump yet, though the day is possibly not far distant when the scorchers will be seen at the tail of the flying pack, just pressing a button as he charges a bullfinch or brook. They will doubtless appear in this guise first in Leicestershire or the Vale of Aylesbury, as there would be a possibility of the wheels clogging, very likely, in the Essex or Oakley clays.

I know it is very irreverent to cast sneers at Dunlops and Coventrys, and I could better endure them if they paid a small duty, which might go to help to defray the cost of the highways they now partly monopolize. There is hardly an M.P. but knows in his heart of hearts this would be equal justice with dog, gun, game, and trap licences, one would imagine; but they must pander to the scorching crowd, or they might be in danger of losing their seats.

I may be an old-fashioned fool and sceptical, but, candidly, I do often harbour a great big doubt whether civilization is much of a boon, after all; whether people are any happier now than they were in the mediæval ages. Statistics don't say we live any longer, and it is questionable whether the old barons and their yeomen and retainers, who hunted, falconed, tilted, drew a longbow, fought their neighbours, lived on venison and salmon, and toasted "fayre ladyes" in flagons of nut-brown October ale, did not enjoy life as much as their descendants of to-day. Menials might have to eat oaten cakes and wild-boar chops, but possibly it did their livers no more harm than Bovril, tinned essence of greasy cart-mare's leg, or German (?) sausage. They missed telegraphy, excursions, and extra special editions, but they comfortably evaded the water-rate man, eight-day summonses, or bogus share lists, and the temptation was not placed under their very noses to lose their money backing "stiff uns" on the tape.

However, it's our bounden duty to accept such entertainment as the gods provide and our tastes incline to, and to extract what fun we can while we sojourn in this vale of tears; and as there are 1000 hunters conditioning in Melton to-day, and Kirby Gate is within very measurable distance, there will be a few more gees bestridden, and a few more novices want lifting in the pigskin, so here goes.

If a boy is hardy and grubs well, as boys generally do, and has plenty of pluck, and keen on it, you may start him riding at seven or eight, but if he is a weakly sort and not over-keen, I should delay his riding a few years later, till he shows an eagerness for it and a desire to follow the hounds. Never frighten a boy by making him ride a horse he seems shy of, or making him ride bareback or without stirrups. Encourage him, but don't force him. Make things as comfortable as you can for him; you can quickly alter his style after a while, when he becomes accustomed to the sensation of riding and has confidence in himself, because this time we are dealing with an "animal" we can instruct by talk and without curbs and martingales. What a job I had to get Frank to bump the saddle, till one day I tied his pony behind a butcher's cart going a twenty-mile round in the country, and told him to "help himself!"

A few hours later, his mother was going up the street, and saw Frank coming back, trotting behind the cart, his face beaming with smiles, and bumping manfully. With a mother's pride, she looked around to admire her boy. Horror of horrors! he had bumped the seat of his knickerbockers clean away, and it was nature's garb that clothed him behind. The mater quickly pursued her way, and disowned him *instanter*. He was her Frank no longer in that uniform.

I hate squibbing ponies for boys to ride hunting on; give me an old hunter that won't put a foot wrong, so long as the child can hold him.

When Frank was nine, he went absolutely straight to hounds on a sixteen-hand horse. His mount had a light mouth, and he rode him in a pretty severe crank-snaffle, as, of course, he had not much strength. I used to make him take hold of his saddle behind with first one hand and then the other as the fences came; that answered the threefold purpose of keeping him from getting a sideways seat, of teaching him to handle his reins and whip in either hand, and from flying about twenty yards over his horse's head, as he must otherwise have done. By degrees he got to take hold occasionally, only at big places and low drops, and as he got older and stronger he left off altogether. Never teach or allow your boy to take hold of his saddle in front under any pretence whatever.

Make a boy ride alternate days or alternate weeks with the whip in reverse hands. Later on, in riding nappy or one-sided horses, or perhaps in finishing a race, he should not experience any more inconvenience from using his whip in one hand than the other. When a horse has a fixed determination to go to the left, and his owner wishes him to go to the right, it looks awfully wooden to see the rider throwing his whip over with his right hand and making futile attempts to hit the horse on the left. One stroke from the whip in the right place and at the right moment has more effect on the horse than twenty wrong ones. A horse lifts the quarter you hit him on; thus, if a horse rears, catch him inside his thigh if you can; and if he kicks, catch him a crack under the jaw.

I am an advocate for the use of the spur, as there are times when you cannot use your whip, but can bring your spur into play. For instance, you are riding a sticky horse at a fence, the beggar is trying to shirk it and bolt either way, and it takes all your two hands to keep him straight. Again, if a horse is rearing, and wants to go his own way, you slide one arm round his neck to avoid pulling him "over end" on you by the bridle, spur him as hard as you can well back and well under the flank on the side you want him to go; that will cause him to turn his quarters from and his head to the road *you* want to go. Be sure and never pull your horse's mouth when he is very straight up, as that causes him to come over on you, and these are nasty dangerous falls. By sliding one arm round the neck you are less likely to drop right under the saddle if you do happen to all come over together; and it is generally the saddle-pommel does the injury when you are come over on.

Let us divide horsemanship under four headings, please—Seat, Hands, Pluck, and Judgment. No man is a perfect horseman who combines any three of these minus the other.

Seat.—The stirrup should be at such a length that the leg from the knee downwards is at about the same degree of perpendicularity as the body. This is a generally accepted old theory which does to work on, but with Archer (my model jockey), who rode extra long, and Tod Sloan riding extra short, one is in a bit of a quandary. Let your boy pupil ride rather long to begin with; he can shorten his leathers a hole or two in a few years if he chooses, there is no set rule. Do not force him to ride with his toe in the stirrup; at present he will feel and be more secure with his foot home in the stirrup, and can practise toe in and heel down, *a la militaire* and the show-ring, later on, and at his leisure.

A graceful seat in the saddle is not to be acquired by rule of thumb—you can't alter formation; but keep your elbows to your side, and your hands down, and your toes not too far stuck out, are useful reminders. Usually a man throws himself too far back when jumping—he should go a little more with his horse; it is tiring to the animal when partially distressed or steeplechasing, and causes it to drag with its hind legs.

Show-ring jumping is a science. Frank can throw himself right back over a low drop, hunting, and throw himself right forward, whilst his head nearly touches his horse's ears when in the air over show fences. Get your show-jumper in mid-air, and you should entirely go forward with him, taking all weight off the hind-quarters, or he may touch with his hind legs, which will lose you the prize in a close competition. Frank rides Topthorne for Mr. Dodsworth of Nottingham (Doddy), so well known, and who has won more jumping prizes than any man living, and knows a bit. I have heard Sir Gilbert Greenall, the present master of the Belvoir, who is a Cheshire man (as is also Dodsworth), say that the latter is the very best man he ever saw to hounds on a rough horse.

Topthorne has won several thousands of pounds in show prizes, but you must go right forward and not touch her mouth one ounce once she rises to her fence, or she will tip with her hind feet. This seat takes some acquiring, and you had better hug the mane a little first time you try it. Once acquired, I believe you can stick on better that way than leaning back, as I have seen Frank come clean through the wall, sometimes on novices, and stop on the pigskin, when I, for one, should have come off. If you do get a fall this way, you have not so far "to come" as when sitting back, and you lose the "chuck" from the horse's quarters, hence the concussion is less; and altogether there is a lot to say for it except at low drops, or when landing into furrows and boggy ground.

You can soon teach a boy from the plough-tail to stick on, because it hurts him to fall, but what is a seat without *hands?* — which denote the artist, and which no one who has started riding late in life can ever acquire. Riding young horses helps to make hands as much as anything; they answer to a "silken thread" pull when their mouths are nicely made. Talk about lifting horses at their fences, as one often hears —stuff and nonsense! Just sit in a clothes-basket and try to lift yourself by the handles, or try playing at horses like children with two strings and a piece of stick in your mouth for a bit. Some one suggests a jump. "All right," you say, "but for goodness' sake don't pull the string when I jump." The hunter would say the same if he could speak.

Mrs. Dudley Smith, who has had such a good season show-jumping on her charming mare Dainty Lass, told me she learnt to loose her hands by riding without any reins at all, and having an attendant to lunge her horse over fences, and I strongly recommend this course of treatment to the bold horsemen who are for ever mauling their horses' heads, and their name is legion.

Mrs. Blockley, who is another fine show-ring lady rider, has not been riding this season; but as her husband has bought Omega, who is the acknowledged champion at the game, she should be in strong evidence next season with him and Alfred, who could win all over with his fair owner for a pilot, but not so with the stable lad up. I expect the latter's hands are too heavy. Ladies generally have good hands, and horses rarely pull at them.

Alfred won £500 show-jumping last year, and £505 the year previous; then one hears people say, "Oh, but my horse is too good for show-jumping!" They are not good enough, they mean. Eight hundred guineas were refused for Alfred two years ago. You might take Tom Firr's stud when in condition, and there would not be a solitary one make a clean round in a show-ring without schooling.

Funny enough, they give the most money for show-jumping all about the Potteries district. There is £100 to be jumped for in two days at Shrewsbury Floral Fête, and £50 in one day at Keele Park, whilst at little village shows they often give £15 and £20 for first prize. The Melton Mowbray Horse Show boldly gives £5 for first prize in this the premier hunting country of the world. "Hooray!" It is nearly all high jumping and no water in Yorkshire, except at the County Show, and all hurdles and water and no gate in Lancashire. You want to place your horse accordingly.

I believe, if you have a very good high jumper, it lowers them an inch or two spreading them at water—at least, it does some. Irrespective of show-jumping, I believe that common-bred horses jump timber better than water. I have seen cart colts stand and jump gates when loose frequently, and quite ponies jump timber splendidly often enough at shows, but they fail at water, and your common horse in the hunting field who makes a brilliant start soon wants his fences "bringing to him" when they run.

I wanted to put one of my little girls up show-jumping this season, as they go quite as well as Frank to hounds, but my wife says she bosses the girls, and wouldn't let me—says I shall be making circus-riders of them, and all sorts of funny things, so I had to give in, as good husbands always do. I thought the judges would be sure to hang a bit to a young girl with her hair down her back. They do hang to the ladies a bit, these judges do, if they get half a chance; and sometimes, when I feel badly treated, I say if we had one lady judge amongst the three, the "mere male" competitor would stand a better chance. I saw it mooted recently in one of the papers that it was in contemplation to organize a sort of central authority to control agricultural and horse shows throughout the country, and I cordially agree with such a movement. It would probably, in a minor degree, bear the same relation to show committees as the jockey club does to local stewards of race meetings, and be a Court of Reference for grievances on the part of exhibitors, with power to blackball fraudulent exhibitors from exhibiting at any show "under the rules."

A big grievance with exhibitors is that some secretaries will take entries with impunity for days after the advertised time of closing, whilst others won't budge an inch. This wants regulating, and there should really be a hard-and-fast rule. Then, again, the want of punctuality is annoying beyond measure. You take a couple of jumpers to a show a hundred miles off, "jumping to take place at 3 p.m.," and make arrangements to get away on business elsewhere or home that night. Probably to suit the convenience of a judge, or from dilatoriness on the part of the stewards, or from some other reason which is no fault of yours, the jumping does not come on till 5 or 6 p.m. Result: another night's expenses and subsequent business arrangements thrown entirely out of gear. Again, I would have a scale of points for judging jumpers, as of a truth the flagrant errors one sees are exasperating beyond measure.

It is impossible to lay down any scale for judging hunters or young stock, so consequently this is the sort of thing one sees, and I can vouch for this case, as I saw it myself this summer: At a certain show there was a class for hunters on the first day, in which A was placed first, and B second, B also taking a first in another class in which A was not entered. Next day, with the same judges, there was a medal or cup for the best of the prize-winners in all classes. They placed B first and A second. As the blackguardly costermonger remarked when his nicely arranged load of vegetables was overturned by a passing hansom, "Well, there *is* no name for this lot!" I suppose the most charitable construction one can place on such a decision is that A had passed a bad night.

When you are showing hunters in a ring, be careful to be guided by this golden rule: keep one eye on your horse, and the other on the judges. Never mind your best girl on the stand or the coach. Nurse and humour your horse so that he may go smoothly and make his best show when the judges' eyes are on him. How tedious it sometimes becomes when judges of hunters ride each selected horse two or three times round the ring! Certainly they should just get up, because no man can properly judge shoulders, balance, and "feel" without; but if they can't tell sufficient for the purpose with one ride round, they are unfitted for their post, and make the whole thing a bore to the occupants of the stand and onlookers generally.

I remember jolly old Sir John Astley having a flutter at the water at the Lincoln County Show once, with a cigar a foot long in his mouth, and a parasol for a whip. Splash he went in the water, and got what looked a fair cropper. After picking himself and the parasol up, it was seen he still had the cigar in his mouth; he had never left go of that. The people did cheer. I believe this yarn is in his book, but I've lent it to somebody who hasn't returned it. Poor Sir John! he was one of the very best of good sorts, and one of a type fast becoming extinct. I knew him well, and heard his memorable speech about Ireland at the Owersley Ram Sale. Some of the Irish members demanded an apology when next the house met, and his reply was, "If they wanted any satisfaction, they could name their own 'tools,'" or something to that effect.

I was helping Sir John one night at one of his election meetings at an awfully radical village. It was when Mr. Laycock knocked him out for North Lincolnshire, and before the "franchise" was extended. They were a terrible rowdy lot at the lower end of the room, and demanded his ideas on extending the franchise. Sir John replied, "I don't mind anybody with any common sense having a vote; but before I'd vote for a lot of hooting, howling devils like you having it, I'd see you all —— first." I thought they would have torn the platform down; it was grand fun, and as we came out of the place they daubed our coats with tarry sticks, etc., and savoury eggs abounded.

I rode home in the brougham with Sir John, who lighted his usual big cigar, and as we neared the end of the village half a brick came sailing clean through both window-panes, and just took the cigar out of his mouth in its course.

He laughed and said, "Not half a bad shot, was it?"

Marvellous to relate, I believe Mr. Chaplin was the only Conservative who kept his seat in Lincolnshire at that time, and the very next general election after the extension of the franchise, they put in nearly all Conservatives and turned the Rads., who had given them the vote, out. *Moral:* When you want something you haven't got, be a Rad. and howl while you get it; but when you've got it, turn a respectable Conservative, and try to keep it.

You can teach a young girl to ride in ever so much less time than you can a boy, because they are so much firmer on their saddles when properly placed. I strongly advocate once more the martingale for ladies, as it is impossible for them, from their high position on the horse, and the saddle-crutch and their knee, to get their hands down as low as a man. There is always the greatest difficulty in getting ladies to keep their shoulders square at first, but the real secret of this is in fixing the foot and stirrup properly. The stirrup should be placed near the toes, only halfway home under the instep, the heel slightly down, and the stirrup tight enough to make the knee as near as possible touch the crutch; then by raising the heel when jumping, or the horse bucking, it fixes the leg in a tight vice under the crutch, and your lady rider takes far more bucking off than a man. If the foot is right home in the stirrup, and the leather a shade too loose, all fixity disappears, the right shoulder goes forward, and the victim of bad teaching twists sideways. Captain Hayes has all these things photographed in his book, and a lot of useful information about ladies' habits, etc. When you are riding behind badly taught ladies, you notice the foot with the toe right down, and the sole of the boot visible behind, and swinging to the motion of the horse.

You can exemplify what I mean as to this power of fixture by sitting in a chair with your foot on the floor and the leg perpendicular. Put weight on the knee where the crutch goes, and endeavour to raise the leg and foot altogether, as you would if the stirrup were right home in the foot, and you will find very small power; but by leaving the toes on the ground as if the stirrup were there, and raising the heel only, you will find you can lift immense pressure—twenty stones easily, I should say.

Properly fixed, you will have very little

difficulty with your lady pupil, and by riding alongside on the off and getting her to keep turning her head towards you, and throwing her left shoulder forward, she will soon sit square. A lady should not make any endeavour to throw herself either backward or forward in leaping, and it is well to just get her to take hold of her saddle behind with her right hand (just linking the fingers under will suffice); then, after the first fence or two, she will go like one o'clock. I remember one of my girls going through quite a good run first time she ever jumped a fence; and last season I taught a lady to ride, and the *sixth* time she was ever in the saddle she followed me with the hounds and jumped quite twenty fences.

It is quite extraordinary the idea some novices have of the simplicity of jumping fences; they get their ideas from pictures and shopkeeper's coloured almanacks. The other day a dream of youth and beauty, to whom I was giving her third lesson, asked me if I thought she could jump quite a young river that flowed by, after a few more lessons. When she was cantering round the corner of the meadow, I asked her to turn "Paddy's" head away from the fence, or very likely he might want to jump it. She replied, "she should love to do that, of all things!" It was a big stake, and bound with an ox-rail in front and a ditch far side. What a fearful responsibility these girls are!

Ladies who ride with the stirrup-leather running round the bar and under the horse, fastening to the saddle on the off side, will require the leather to be drawn tighter when they have been on some little time, as the horse's back goes down and the girths relax. I am in favour of this adjustment, as by pulling from the far side it helps to keep the saddle in place. Where a safety bar and fixed stirrup only is used, the girths will still require tightening, or sore backs will ensue. My girls ride any fresh horses I happen to buy straight off; I never find the horses take much exception to the novelty. But there is just a danger of a horse rolling when standing about the first few times, with the extra tightness of ladies' girths and the novel pressure of the stirrup-girth, which is further back than they have been accustomed to.

My third essential towards the "complete horseman," viz. *Pluck*, conveys its own meaning pretty well. If you are short of it you can buy some—

not in the form of penny packets at the chemist's, though; it is sold in bottles and by the glass at hotels and other dens of iniquity, and is called "cherry brandy," "orange gin," "mountain dew," and by various other well-known titles. But these bought varieties evaporate quickly, leaving the patient weak and debilitated, and I should strongly advise such as are minus the real article to ride bikes, or, what may be preferable in such case, tricycles; or, perhaps even better still, to run a sturdy cob in a tub-cart, with suitable refreshments for the hungered and athirst who have been riding nasty horrid horses. I think nerve is really a better term than pluck, as the latter is liable to be there without the former, something after this kind. Pluck and Nerve come up together in a nasty ugly corner, having chanced to get wide of the rest of the field, with a regular yawner ahead and no option but to have a flutter.

After a cursory glance from both, "Pluck" rams his hat tight, and with a "Here goes the last of the Cardigans" sort of air, flails his horse at it at a tremendous pace (right off his legs, in fact), and, just failing to reach the far bank, takes an imperial cropper the other side. "Nerve," who had simultaneously taken his own line, gliding up to another part of the fence, and holding his gee well together for a final effort, and, with just one reminder as he rose to the occasion, lands by the skin of his teeth, but with nothing to spare.

There are hundreds, and even thousands of men who, having the first three of my qualifications in a more or less degree, are almost utterly devoid of

Judgment. To commence with, they gallop most of the way to cover on their first horse, who (sweating freely) they let stand at the cover corner, for they were late at the meet, and he contracts a chill to start the day with. As soon as hounds run, they continually jump the wrong side of every fence that faces them at right angles, taking on the plough where they might have had the grass. With hounds feathering half a field ahead, and a doubt as to whether they had run heel a few yards, they go blundering over the wide drain with the rotten bank far side a little to the left. They are no sooner over than the second whip's halloa back to the right compels them to jump back, with the rotten bank on the take-off side. They never pick the furrow down the long plough-field; they bucket their horse the first quarter of an hour, and are never by any chance seen at the end of a long straight run. A ringing fox suits them best. They arrive home with their gee in a lather in the evening, and curse their stud-groom on Sunday mornings because the horses' coats are "staring."

Before concluding this chapter I have just a word to say about shoeing hunters. I am not going to enter into elaborate details as to open heels promoting the growth of the frog, etc., as that is more at home perhaps in a veterinary work; but what I wish to impress is the desirability of having a small, neat, sharp cork-ing on the outside hind shoe. I am certain it saves many a fall. I should never dream of jumping in a show-ring without either frost-nails or screw cork-ings. Horses can't jump when they can't hold their feet; and although some slip very much more than others, it is wise to take this preventative, especially in a grass country, where the going is often very greasy and slippery.

CHAPTER V

FOR'ARD AWAY

I was duly entered to hounds at the age of eight in the Burton country in Lincolnshire, which at that time also included the present Blankney country, and would stand eight or nine days a week comfortably, being of vast area and dotted with some of the finest strongholds for the vulpine race to be found in these isles. From that day to this I have steadfastly, and without one moment's doubt, entertained the belief that fox-hunting was the best fun under the broad canopy of heaven, the healthiest pastime, the field in which the most lasting friendships are cemented, and in which the best instincts of the *genus homo* are fostered. A manly sport in which peer and peasant participate on a level footing, and which leaves no disagreeable after-taste.

The Burton country has been hunted by some of the most illustrious masters whose names adorn the pages of hunting lore: Osbaldeston, Assheton Smith, Sir Richard Sutton, and (at the time I entered, and not the least notable) old Lord Henry Bentinck. He was a marvellous man. He would ride thirty miles from Welbeck of a morning, hunt all day, and go like blazes, and at odd times has been known to hack back at night. Being somewhat of a martyr to gout, he ate only one meal a day, and hated women and Sundays—the latter because it deprived him of a seventh part of his hunting. He was a shrivelled, thin, hard-looking, little old man, and I have never yet set eyes on another who looked so much as if he had been born on horseback, and never been off all his life.

He had a very squeaky voice; and many's the time I and some mates have galloped past him on our ponies in a muddy ride, and splashed him well on purpose to hear him swear. He used to sort of squeal the words out; it was lovely to hear them float on the breeze as we made tracks round the corner pretty sharp. He was a gallant and enthusiastic old sportsman, and rode the very best of blood-hunters of the compact type. Lord Henry died at Tathwell, an outlying estate of Mr. Chaplin's, after shooting one day; and there was not a particle of food inside him at the autopsy—he literally died of starvation through being over-abstemious. Mr. Chaplin hunted the whole country after Lord Henry's death, and soon after that it was divided.

I quite agree with what Cusstance says in his delightful book, that Mr. Chaplin was the best welter-weight he ever saw cross a country. He must have ridden some seventeen stones in those days, and never swerved from his line an inch, always riding grand weight-carriers. It's very notable how a man who can afford it, and is a judge, sets up a special type of hunter as his fancy dictates.

Lord Lonsdale had my *beau ideal* type of Leicestershire hunter, both for himself and the Quorn-hunt servants. Big reaching blood-horses, with bone that for appearance would not have been disgraced in a Grand National field. They were nearly all dark chestnuts, with hog manes and long tails. Undocked horses are all the rage just now—it's the whim of the hour; and I see the Hunter's Improvement Society have laid down a law that all foals are to be undocked henceforth and for ever.

Most little men like an upstanding blood-horse (think it gives them a more commanding appearance, I suppose), but there are exceptions; and Captain Warner, ex-master of the Quorn, and Mr. Henry Milner, are two I call to mind who generally rode rather undersized horses from choice. I notice the Duke of Marlborough, who hunts here, is going in entirely for greys. Nothing carries "pink" to greater advantage than a white grey, in my opinion; but being a little conspicuous, you are always liable to be chaffed by your friends if you have hoisted the "white feather" on the white horse "within sight."

You want a shorter-coupled horse in a heavy clay country, and where there is a superabundance of plough, than in galloping grass countries like Leicestershire and Meath, where speed is so highly essential. I must admit to liking a hunter with a fair amount of action in his trot, and, although a thorough horseman can enjoy a run on a ewe-necked one, or one which carries his head right near the ground, providing it goes on, stays, and keeps jumping clean all day, it is really pleasanter riding a horse which, without being peacocky, carries its head well up. I like a horse you can "see coming a good long way off" when he is walking or trotting towards you.

I must take this opportunity to correct an erroneous impression pretty widely in circulation, to the effect that weedy horses which look incapable of carrying a medium-weight man will do to carry a lady. Nothing of the sort. Ladies take more carrying than men, and want strong-backed horses. In the first place, their saddles are far heavier; but it is the fact that they are all the time in one position, and the weight concentrated on one particular pressure, that tires so much. A man turns half round often enough, and sits on one thigh occasionally, stands in his stirrups at times, and frequently, and with good judgment, too, gets off his horse altogether after a short burst for a few minutes. Every shooting-man knows what a relief it is to set down one's gun at lunch-time, or to change shoulders, or hand to a servant after standing long at the cover corner; so it is a relief to the hunter to have the weight relieved or set down for a while; but ladies' hunters get none of this, so we may at once dispel the idea that weak-backed weeds are any good for them to ride.

Referring for a moment further still to ladies' hunters, it is highly essential their heads should be set at the right angle. Boring and ewe-necked and high-backed horses give a most uncomfortable sensation to a lady from her high position on the saddle, and give an impression to them that they will be off over their heads unless they are careful. Get a horse with his head nicely "set on," not "hung on," his shoulders well placed, and his back and loins strong, but not unduly high, and you have a model-topped horse for a lady.

Shoulders are far the most difficult

part of a hunter to judge. Many people think that if a horse has a high thin wither, his shoulders are lovely, but that does not follow at all. Thin withers are usually weak, and I don't mind some little thickness and a trifle of width there, so long as the shoulder goes well back at top; it only denotes strength. The shoulder-point should be fairly forward, and well defined, and must not give the appearance from the front view of being what we call "bullock-chested." Standing at the side, look where the girth will sit; there must be depth and fullness here in the heart place, and a horse in condition must carry the girth well back from his elbows, or else there is something wrong with the mechanism, and they won't work with that elasticity which gives such a delightful ride.

A horse with good shoulders and good

galloping quarters is a long horse with a short back. His length wants to be derived from his quarters and the placing of the shoulders. Let a man fancy himself ever so good a judge of shoulders, he cannot quite tell how the machinery will work till he gets up. Then you will soon know, especially if you ride over ridge and furrow or downhill.

In buying horses off a dealer, a gentleman has so many more facilities for trial than he has in buying one by auction at the Repository, in which case, unless he happens to know the horse, he is working blindfold as to his manners and capabilities. A dealer, however, who buys at the Repository has many strings to his bow. If he buys a horse to suit a certain customer, and it fails to hit the mark, it will doubtless suit some one else. Moreover, the gentleman who buys off a dealer can, as a rule, on finding the horse hardly fulfils expectations in some trifling way, exchange it for another, but not so at the Repository. I am quite certain that, without the slightest exaggeration, I frequently see horses knocked down at 200 and 300 guineas at the Repository sales that, if brought back the following week under another name, but with every imaginable guarantee it is possible to devise, would not make thirty-five guineas. Gentlemen buy owners' names, not the horse, at the Repository. I have had some capital deals out of Repository horses, and no end of bad ones.

Here's a case of how prices fluctuate without any apparent cause. A year last spring a horse called Bantam went up in a swell stud from Melton to the Leicester Repository, and was sold for

180 guineas. In the autumn he came up to the same place again, with the same description exactly, and I bought him for 15 guineas. This is the horse Frank rode his first chase at Leicester, as previously recorded, and I sold him after the race for 48 guineas. Last week "as ever was," he came again to the Leicester Repository and made 148 guineas; and cheap enough, too, as there are few better hunters, and he is quite one of the right sort to look at.

About four years ago I bought a great banging four-year-old, also at Leicester, and also at 15 guineas. He had no description except his pedigree; and whilst being shown he took the liberty of playfully kicking the rail in half just near the rostrum, and only just missed my head. I suppose that was partly why he came so cheap. He was a comical-tempered beggar at first, but soon came to all right, and we hunted him a bit; and finding he was useful, I ran him in a hunt steeplechase within six weeks. A gentleman's son who lives not a thousand miles from here saw him one day, and bought him off me for £80, if he passed his vet., and I sent the horse over to be examined next day; but he came back with a most insulting letter from the buyer, asking me what I took him for, and all that sort of thing, and declaring I must have known the horse made a noise, and enclosing V.S. certificate to that effect. Two or three days after, I knocked up against another gentleman in the Birdcage at Newmarket, who, having seen him run in the steeplechase, asked me the price, and I said £130. He said, "Well, I'll take him if he passes ——," naming one of the leading Newmarket vets. I saw the horse examined, and was somewhat relieved when, after giving him a rare pipe-opener, the vet. pulled up, saying, "Well, he's sound in his wind; that's one thing." He passed all right, and so it was not an ill wind that blew my first customer to one side. Last time I saw the gentleman who bought the horse, he asked me if I had some more like him, as he had sold him for £450.

I am not a V.S., but I have more confidence in my own trial of wind than theirs, with a few exceptions I know of. In its incipient stages, you cannot always detect roaring from a strong gallop. Merely the gentlest canter down a shady hedge-side, so the rustle of the wind doesn't drown it, and in other cases the "band won't play" without extreme exertion. Tracheotomy is useful for chasers, and has beneficial effect, but it is too big a nuisance for the ordinary hunter.

The very grandest stud of weight-carriers I ever saw were the late Marquis of Waterford's, who came over to Brocklesby to stay with Lord Yarborough when the agrarian malcontents stopped hunting in his own country and drove him and his hounds away. A wonderful, chatty, nice man Lord Waterford was, with all the characteristic gameness of the Beresfords in him. I was farming just inside the Burton country, on the borders of the Brocklesby, at that time, and the Burton met at my house once a month or so.

One day Lord Waterford came over to hunt with the Burton with us, and we had the fastest twenty-five minutes on record from Fen Wood back to my place. The beaten fox tried to scale the high garden wall, but the leading hound pulled him back by the tag. However, after a roll over, he succeeded in scaling the wall, and the hounds, all following, clean knocked over two young children of mine who were at play the other side. We killed the fox in the garden, and Lord Waterford "blooded" those two young ones, who, I regret to record, both died of diphtheria a couple of years later. I have kept that fox's mask, although I have been sold up stick and stone once or twice since then. No man is fonder of his children than I, and out of fifteen I still have eleven amongst which to divide my affections.

There's another fox's mask facing me as I write—a memento of the very best run I ever saw. It was in the winter of '79-80. We had two tremendous long frosts, with an interval of about two weeks between, and I never saw hounds run as they did those two weeks. They met at my house again on this occasion; and, after a muddling gallop from my cover in the morning, we found another fox in a small cover not far away. I have never seen a fox break cover before or since as this old warrior did—not creeping out, as foxes generally do; he flew the stake and bound hedge half-way down the cover at a bound, and made straight for the open.

We made a fourteen-mile point on the map, and killed beyond Brigg. It was a lovely kill in the centre of a big grass-field, and we numbered seven all told. Will Dale, the huntsman, Joe Clixby, and I jumped the last fence abreast just as they pulled this best of good foxes down. "The brush, Will!" we simultaneously cried; but it was a dead heat, so we tossed. Of course I lost, so Joe took the brush, and I the mask. Poor Billy Parr, a friend who has since joined the majority, rolled over down the railway bank just before we finished, and knocked his teeth out on the metals.

I rode a small blood mare through this run that looked quite two stone under my weight, and the ground was very heavy, but she kept skimming along as only blood ones can. Who has not experienced this pleasing sensation, when hounds have been running an hour, and the common-bred horse is in a ditch-bottom, and has to be flogged out, while your better-bred one manages to negotiate those trappy places with ever a leg to spare?

Only four days after this great run we had another almost as good, getting right into a country where hounds had never been seen before, finishing at Messingham, near the Trent. Mr. Foljambe was master in those days— quite a model of the fine old English gentleman of the old school, not the class who thought it the exclusive privilege of their high office to "blow a horn and curse their friends," as an old adage says, but the acme of courtesy and good sportsmanship combined. One of his ancestors used to hunt in a trap after he was blind, and it is said that he knew the note of every individual hound perfectly.

Old Colonel Forester, the father of the Melton hunt, if not of the Turf as well, up to his decease last year, was not far short of being blind, but he went great guns to the finish, and led his second horseman (who rode close up) a rare dance, as he couldn't see what he was riding at, and didn't care much, either.

What a game old boy he was, to be sure!

Will Dale, our huntsman, who is now with the Badminton, was absolutely the finest man I ever saw cross a country, and the best huntsman into the bargain. It was a sight to be remembered to see the quick, smart way in which he would come out of Wickenby Wood with twenty couple, almost atop of his fox. This said Wickenby Wood was a rare fox-stronghold, and in Lord Henry's time was never once drawn blank in ten seasons. There's Stainton Wood, too, not far off, a marvellous home for foxes. I remember one New Year's Eve we ran into it late in the afternoon, and counted thirteen foxes on foot.

Dale said, if there was only a moon, he'd have hunted the old year out and the new year in. Next morning (New

Year's Day), I so well remember, we met at Clay Bridge, where I was married, and, finding in this same cover in three minutes, ran a sixteen-mile point to Normanby-on-the-Wolds, where I was born.

I was very nearly completing the "treble event" by being buried in that run, too, within a mile or two of the finish, as my mare, who was getting very beaten, put her foot in a rabbit-hole, cantering alongside a deep narrow brook. We turned a somersault, and I lay under the mare on my back, who was also on her back. My legs were jammed, and they daren't lift the mare for fear she should damage me in her struggles; so I lay, with the water running down my back, in the cooling stream, whilst they dug the bank away and hauled me out. From that day to this

I have, periodically, the most excruciating muscular rheumatism and lumbago—but less often as time goes on.

Will Dale's motto was, "Best fox first away, and after him as quick as you can." His hounds always displayed that very good sign of seeming so fond of him, and, my word, didn't he take some stopping! Such a cheery chap, too, he was, and always a pleasant word for the country-people—which goes a long way. If you want to make hunting popular, give the madding crowd on foot and wheels a show now and then, when circumstances seem to demand; you don't lose much. I don't believe in the autocratic master who is for ever trying to elude a few onlookers.

I saw the other day, in the memoirs of Bismarck (most patriotic of statesmen), that he was credited with the remark that the happy moments of our life, all told, didn't amount to twenty-four hours. Bismarck, though, had never tasted the sweets of riding our vale after an afternoon fox, with a few remnants of the field and Will Dale, or he would never have given expression to this belief.

For one hour and fifty minutes over a grand country, nearly a straight line, and all the fences wanting jumping! Lovely to see those bitches work and drive! Now they twist and turn. Our fox is sinking, and he's out of his latitude. Yonder he goes, Will, in the grass-field on the hillside, by the clump of trees. We must have this brook. Hold up, old man! That's over; but there's more to come that will stand no liberties, and still they're running on. He sobs and reaches, does my generous steed, but he's by Chanticleer, dam by old Harkaway, and very fit. Who-whoop at last! Those were halcyon days! Why, oh, why will they not return?

I am not too ambitious, but without some of that commodity you're nowhere. I have no ardent ambition to be a millionaire. There have been four or five of those jokers either commit suicide or gone broke this very year. I entertain a strong conviction that the happiest are those who just acquire a nice little bit more wealth than they start with, and not too much. About £20,000 would fit me to a nicety, and back in the old home. The little farmer of 100 acres who presently becomes master of 200 acres is happy; so is the mechanic or artisan who builds a house and pays for it, or who, having two or three houses, plays them up into a nice little row of houses. Not much pleasure in owning houses, to my mind. You can't ride 'em, and they won't jump a country. Tastes differ, and a good job too.

But to return to the hunting. I remember a funny thing happening one day to Dale and myself. We were walking over a high arched old brick bridge, going to draw Buslingthorpe Wood. When on the top the old bridge broke in, and we all went splash into the water with eight or nine couple of hounds. My word, what a clatter and a splash there was! I came out of the water and *débris* with his horse one side, and he came out with mine the other. Nobody hurt much, though, and it's all in the fun. Dale got very few falls, but pretty bad ones when he did; always stuck on as long as he could, if it was in a brook-bottom.

I remember one morning he came to

my place to go and have a day with the Brocklesby, and he remarked, "This is my 101st day out this season, and I haven't had a fall yet." Shortly after this he broke his thigh very badly. Good horsemen don't get many falls, but have to take their whack as the fickle goddess dictates.

Mr. Shrubb—another master, who now hunts a pack down South—was a good-hearted sort of man, and his only crime was that he was born south of the Thames, which—ridiculous as it may seem—is unpardonable in the eyes of some north-countrymen. He had a ringing voice, very well calculated, like John Peel's, either to "awaken the dead, or the fox from his lair in the morning."

Mr. Wemyss, who hunted our country twice, and was quite young when he came the first time, was just the most reckless horseman I ever set eyes on. He'd a heart as big as the proverbial bucket, and pluck by the cart-load. He used to start off cubbing soon after twelve midnight, and land home to kennel about four the following afternoon, looking fresh. He would take his five or six falls daily, and seem to revel in them, but toned down a lot later on, and was quite a model M.F.H. I should like to see him back in the old country again. We had an extraordinary good run cubbing one day during his *régime*, running from Magin Moor to Ingleby, quite a ten-mile point. I and some friends had been shooting all day before, playing cards all night, and took this lot on before breakfast, so that was quite a good innings.

Some men take no pleasure in cubbing. Too slow, they say; don't care for it till the opening meet. With such I have no sympathy. There's pleasure in knowing where cubs abound, and in seeing the young entry take to their quarry, and in getting your new purchase from Tattersall's nicely to your hand; while to one who loves and admires nature, what is more beautiful than woodland scenery bathed in richest autumn colours and tints, and the awakening of bird and animal life as cheerily breaks the smiling morn? The man who trudges from his cradle to his grave, blind or indifferent to the impressive beauty of nature, misses something, and for such a one I have lumps of pity and a smattering of contempt.

I generally had one or two farming pupils about this time, and we enjoyed life immensely, hunting, shooting, and coursing, and the good things of this life in general. One of these said pupils was a rum fellow—of town the towniest. As soon as he could hold on over a fence at all, we took him out hunting, of course. Bond Street had turned him out regardless, but taking five croppers the first day like a man rather upset him, and coupled with the fact that he had taken sundry neat brandies *en route*, he was a nice object when we started for home. Oh, what a cold night that was! so we called at a good-hearted farmer's for some more brandy. I think he mixed the brandy with gin instead of water, as it sat very warm and comforting. Walking up the next hill, I noticed our hero beginning to wobble a bit, and when we arrived at the top he muttered, "Letsh rache!" and over the hedge he went, we after him. There was a gorse cover two fields ahead, but he never saw it, and we shouted, "Go on, Charlie;

you'll win!" His mare jumped the fence, and stopped short in the ride, and I can see Charlie's legs and coat-tails now, as he took a header into the gorse and bramble bush. We got the remains home somehow, but he was in sticking-plaster for many days. Charlie's father was connected with the Turkish embassy in some way, and the sultan sent him over a small sack of the most lovely tobacco, which landed ultimately at our place. I have respected the sultan ever since, in spite of the very playful manner in which he humbugs our Foreign Office.

Red-letter days used to come thick and fast, and what fun we had one spring with the puppies! I reckon my father and I have just about walked a pack of hounds, but I have been most unlucky in getting runners with the pack—distemper, twisted legs, or something always sure to go wrong. However, at this time I had a couple showed a delightful capability to hunt any mortal thing, and as three or four neighbours had some too, we used to make a pack, assisted by three or four shepherd dogs, and about a dozen terriers. We generally hunted a drag, but more often hares, and one day, I blush to relate, we had twenty-five minutes after a fox. Of course, we had a horn, and all that, but they were a most unruly crew. The end of that pack was that two or three malcontents, headed by a neighbouring parson, who farmed his own glebe, advertised in the local paper, warning off all persons and dogs other than those who hunted with a *recognized pack*.

Two of the best sporting farmers in our country were Mr. Carnley, father of the present owner of Norbury Squire, and Mr. William Nicholson of Willoughton. They both rode in well-weathered scarlet and hunting-caps. Mr. Carnley would ride his fifteen miles to cover, and hunt all day, not distressing himself much; but let hounds run towards Torrington of an afternoon, and see if he wouldn't be there! He was one of the cleverest at a tricky place I ever saw. Old Lord Henry always asserted Mr. Nicholson was the best man he ever set eyes on to hounds.

Speaking of hunting-caps, what a comfort they are compared to the abominable pot-hat! but nothing else is admissible now, and you must be fashionable or you are nowhere, especially in this metropolis of hunting, where it is terribly *infra dig.* to evince even the least enthusiasm after anything. If you have had the run of the season, the most you may utter is, "Not bad gallop" or "Decent thing;" and if you pass a fellow going to cover who tells you he has got a "fresh crock"—gave Hughie Overton £600 for it the night before last at Spider's dinner, the most you must say is, "Ah! useful sort of beast." So wags the world and the people in it, and there's a ruling fashion even in a shake of the hand or the way in which you say ta-ta.

Kirby Gate, the time-honoured meet which heralds the Leicestershire hunting season, is a sight for the gods: 500 horsemen mounted on such cattle as you could not see excelled anywhere in the wide world, their masters irreproachably tailored and groomed; about 100 of the fairest of the fair, the majority in their pale-blue silk Quorn Hunt collars, with just a fetching peep of scarlet waistcoat.

As this "glad throng goes marching along" from Kirby Gate to Gartree Hill, they are accompanied by a tremendous string of traps of every conceivable description, extending some miles, amid clouds of foot-people.

Tom Firr, the Quorn huntsman, is a man who stands right out by himself, so to speak, and I look upon him as quite one of the institutions of the country, he has hunted so long and with such marked ability; a perfect horseman and huntsman, who, although he has faced the music so many seasons, and had so many bad falls, goes as well as the best of them yet.

The difficulty of hunting a country like this is naturally very much enhanced by the crowd being so great, and the crush on leaving cover in the Monday and Friday country is fearful. There is no breathing-room, and till you get quit of the surging mass you are continually getting wedged and jostled—most likely by some over-fed stockbroker who subscribes his 250 guineas or perchance his 25 guineas per annum to the fund. All right, my particular old enemy, I'm well charged with a fresh volley of expletives for the season, and next time you shove me on to the catch of the gate or cut in at the only gap, there'll be music in the air.

There are but two classes of society who can really afford to be totally independent, viz. those who have more money than they know what to do with, and those who have none; and this pet aversion of mine and myself are fair examples of both.

The country here (except the glorious Vale of Belvoir) is so undulating that unless you are almost on the top of the hounds you can't see them work, and that to my mind is a deprivation of one of the principal charms of the chase. Out of a field of 500 here, though, I don't suppose more than about 100 care a hang what the hounds are hunting, and another hundred would prefer they never found at all. Still, there are a few who really go, and don't *half* go, either; but the majority are assisting only at a social function, inhaling pure oxygen, and getting an appetite for their dinners.

A young swell is hardly properly entered till he has done a Melton season, I presume; but for young Archibald, Plantagenet, Trevelyan, Browne (son of old Jasper Brown, of Peckham Rye), I should recommend Leamington, Cheltenham, or Leighton Buzzard. We are a bit ultra down here, but less so than of old, and likely to get less so still, as the world gets more democratic every day, and there's a beastly commercialism in the air, breathe where one may.

I've just remembered a yarn about old Bob Oliver, a gruff, hard-riding old farmer, who farmed his own land, had hunted three or four days a week all his life, was undisturbed by mortgages or overdrafts, and not overburdened with civility or courtesy.

One day there appeared on the scene Lord Wodehouse of Wodehouse, who was staying with Squire A. in the Brocklesby country. Hounds found in due course, and it was easy to see by the way they spoke and ran it was a scenting morning, and a good run was in store. Lord Wodehouse of Wodehouse blocked the way at the gate at the end of the ride, and after several wasted seconds in a futile attempt on his part to open it, Bob (whose patience was exhausted) gave him a bit of a shove, and said, "For God's sake let somebody come as can undo it." When they ultimately pulled down their fox, his lordship asked his host, Squire A., who that disagreeable old chap was. The reply was, "Oh, only old Bob Oliver— rare old sportsman, but a bit odd; wants handling, that's all." His lordship, thinking to put matters right, went up to our hero and said, "Mr. Oliver, I believe; and I'm pleased to make your acquaintance; but really you were a bit rough on me coming out of the wood this morning, but perhaps you might not know I'm Lord Wodehouse of Wodehouse, and staying at the Hall." Bob stared a second or two, and then said, "You may be Lord Wodehouse of Wodehouse, or you may be Lord Outhouse of Outhouse, for aught

I know, but you're a damned bad hand at a gate."

This took place thirty-five years ago up our way, and I saw it repeated in the *Sporting Times* a year or two ago. I've the greatest respect for the Pink Un, where one sees a new-laid joke worth repeating occasionally, and the soundest and best of Turf lore.

Mr. Rawnsley, Master of the Southwold, is quite one of the most successful amateur huntsmen of the day, and has carried the horn now many seasons. The Southwold is a good sporting country, and I used to hunt with them generally one or two days a week years ago, notably during Captain Fox's mastership, with old Dan Berkshire as huntsman. Dan had a rare voice, but always seemed in a bustle; he was remarkably clever, though, at hunting the big woods on the Linwood side of the country. Captain Fox was always well mounted on a good class of horse, but never jumped the nasty obstacles. He was the most courteous of men, and would raise his hat to a tramp if the tramp raised his.

Speaking of amateur huntsmen (who are not always an unmixed blessing), we must not omit Mr. J. Maunsell Richardson of Brocklesby fame, dual winner of the Grand National on Disturbance and Reugny, one of the best cross-country gentlemen riders at that time, quite one of the nattiest and best all-round horsemen in England to-day. After winning his last National on Reugny, whom he trained himself in Brocklesby Park, there was a split in the stable camp over which Captain Machell was the presiding genius, and Mr. Richardson relinquished silk for e'er and aye. Later on he married Victoria, Countess of Yarborough, and has hunted periodically, and been alternately field-master of, the Brocklesby hounds ever since.

Old Mr. Alec Goodman was likewise one of the foremost gentlemen riders of his day, and is now quite an old man. I saw him going wonderfully well to hounds, though, only a few years ago. He won three Grand Nationals, on Salamander, Miss Mowbray, and Alcibiade, I think, without reference. He invariably made the running, and rode twenty-eight times over the Liverpool Grand National course without a fall—a truly marvellous and unique performance, and a contrast in horsemanship to some examples here, where you can see five-and-twenty falls in five-and-twenty minutes any hunting morning from Walton Thorns or Holwell Mouth. I know three generations of Alec

Goodmans now living, and gave young Alec, the grandson, his first mount on a horse I ran at Huntingdon about four years ago.

Everybody ought to see the Brocklesby hounds, which are, if I remember rightly, the oldest-established pack in the world. The Belvoir and they are certainly the two best-looking packs in the kingdom. Racing-like hounds, with lovely shoulders, all quality, and alike as peas. The Oakley are a grand pack, and well adapted to their heavy holding country. They are big strong hounds, with big limbs, and must be a standard higher than the Belvoir, and not their equal in colour, which is incomparable.

I have had several very enjoyable runs with Mr. Green's stag-hounds near Bury St. Edmunds, over the heavy Suffolk bank country. Suffolk is a county so much devoted to game that stag-hunting is a good substitute for fox-hunting, though the latter is carried on under difficulties by the Suffolk and the Newmarket and Thurlow fox-hounds. Stag-hunting in Suffolk, with its heavy clay, is indeed a contrast to stag-hunting over Aylesbury Vale, where the Rothschilds pack lead their many followers. Stag-hunting is rare good fun, but more artificial than fox-hunting, and I prefer the latter. If one mentions stag-hunting to an old-fashioned fox-hunter of the calibre of Mr. Foljambe, for instance, one's remarks are accepted with chilly courtesy, the while a tiny cynical smile plays in the corners of his mouth.

CHAPTER VI

THE NOBLE ART OF BACKING WINNERS ON THE TURF

ONLY to think this is the last chapter! Oh, happy thought! Never, when I started, did I ever think I should struggle through, but somehow, whilst writing of riding and hunting matters, I seemed to glide along glibly enough. Beyond doubt, should this book ever see the inside of a cover, it will be handed down to posterity as the greatest jumble ever written. I am fully aware things are dotted down in one chapter which belong to another, and so on, but any attempt at revision or classification is ten times more irksome, I find, than coming from pillar to post with one run *a la* Tod Sloan ; and as this young gentleman is creating quite a *furore* throughout this country from one end to the other just now, and creating a greater stir in sporting circles than any jockey has done since Archer's day, it may be as well just to criticize him to start with.

I have closely studied Sloan's mode of procedure, from mounting to dismounting, and have come to the conclusion that he is undoubtedly a fine horseman, as far as being on good terms with his horse and his hands are concerned. In the first place, he is averse to tight-girthing when first the saddle is put on, and as this often takes place some twenty minutes before it is necessary to get up, there's reason in it. He usually gives his horse a familiar pat when mounted; and, when cantering down to the post, sits as still as a mouse, and does not maul his head about, as one so often sees done. I am prepared to admit there is ground for the contention that there is less resistance to the wind-pressure when sitting in his crouching attitude than straight up, but I do not attribute this or the concentration of weight on the horse's withers to his remarkable success, so much as his judgment of pace, his quick beginning, and letting them come along. Whilst I very much doubt his control over wayward horses is so great, sitting where he does, as where our jockeys sit, I am also dubious as to its efficacy when coming downhill. We should see this tested more fully on courses like Epsom and Brighton, and, so far, I am not aware that Sloan has performed on any but flat or uphill courses like Sandown, in which latter case I should deem it an advantage having weight forward, but not so round Tattenham Corner. It will be remembered that, in riding Asterie second in the Cesarewitch the other day, the mare, after going well at the bushes, seemed to falter coming down the slight gradient known as Bushes Hill, but strode away again with greater freedom up from the Abingdon Mile bottom. Weight forward is sound argument going uphill, but may it not hamper a horse and upset his balance going down one? That being for ever held back, having to come round beaten horses, and getting shut in, are some of the penalties these always-waiting, flash-finishing crack jockeys have to pay is quite in the order of things, and a policy which merits the reward it often meets.

I remember Sims, the darkey jockey,

who is Sloan's principal rival in America, coming over three or four years ago. He rode, like Sloan, right on the withers, and came all the way. I think the first race he won was on Eau Gallie in the Crawford Plate at the Newmarket Craven Meeting. I had a horse running, and was on the trainer's stand in the Birdcage to watch the race. Sims was off quick, and soon held a long lead, seeming to be niggling slightly at his horse all the way. All round they kept saying, " He'll come back to them;" but not he—they held him too cheaply, and he won comfortably at the finish.

I am aware a jockey can't come without his horse, but when they won't come with it when they can, just to gain public applause for winning a short head with a well-timed finish, as the papers say, then just get beaten, they deserve it; but what about the owner and trainer and the unfortunate backer? If you study and take note of the report in which such a jockey as I have indicated (who never will come along without most emphatic orders, and not always then) finishes in the first two, you will find "just failed to get up, and was beaten a head" is more often recorded than "won by a head on the post."

I believe it to be a common fallacy amongst trainers and jockeys that because a horse is top weight in a handicap he should necessarily be held back and waited with, as is generally done. The said horse has displayed merit, and shown some previous form to place him in the position of top weight amongst his rivals, and by keeping him back I contend that you deny him the opportunity to bring his merit into play until the last final dash, to say nothing of the mauling he gets in the effort to control him.

Archer is my "best jockey." No man ever came round Tattenham Corner with greater resolution than he. George Fordham was probably his equal on straight courses; and that neatest of jockeys, Tom Cannon, was a champion at coaxing a green two-year-old; but Archer must be my "all round" man. He invariably got off, and was a perfect judge of pace, finished with undeniable determination and ability, and won at the post where stands the umpire whose decision settles the fortune of so many thousands.

I was well placed for an unofficial judge when Melton and Paradox finished for the Derby. Archer, who rode Melton, was fifteen inches behind two lengths from the post. By what seemed almost a superhuman effort, he was fifteen inches in front passing the post, whilst the next stride placed Paradox again in the van. I didn't measure the inches, but this imaginary illustration may serve to convey my meaning.

Jimmy Snowden was another brilliant horseman when sober, and not so bad when he wasn't, and I was an ardent admirer of his riding.

I remember a match between Archer on Knight of Burghly and Snowden on Lock Leven at Manchester. It was quite a sporting affair, and after both jockeys riding for all they were worth, one won by a head, but for the life of me I can't remember which just now, and as I've never made a reference of any sort since I started, I'm not going to begin now. It's too much worry, and what little hair there is left on my cranium is fast going grey.

I spoke to Archer on Newmarket heath during exercise hours the morning of Sailor Prince's Cambridgeshire (that was about a fortnight before his death), and, upon my word, he had wasted to such an extent and got so thin you could as near as possible count his ribs through his covert coat. Archer had laid himself out with extra determination to win the Cambs. on St. Mirin that day, but the coup was not destined to be realized, for though the "all scarlet" was prominent at the red post—that well-known landmark on the then Cambs. course, now known as the Old Cambs. course—after a desperate struggle, in which Archer (in a weak state, and hampered by a broken stirrup-leather, hardly showed, it was thought, his accustomed brilliancy) succumbed by a head to Sailor Prince, ridden by "Tiny" White.

Archer hunted a good deal in Leicestershire, and I have it on the undeniable authority of Tom Firr that he was a nailing good man to hounds; so is his brother, C. Archer, as I can vouch by personal observation.

What on earth becomes of all the light-weight jockeys who take the sporting world by storm for a season or so, and afterwards vanish into oblivion? You can see scores of their names if you look through some old calendars, whom you remember as having created a small *furore* at some particular time, and you had forgotten such ever existed till your memory is suddenly refreshed. I suppose a lot of them go to the bad; the temptation held out to these youngsters and the glamour of their position ruin them.

A few years ago the Jockey Club raised the scale of weights from a minimum of

5 st. 7 lbs. to 6 st., and I should like to see it raised higher still, as common sense tells us a 6-st. boy can have very little control over a strong wilful horse; then, of what use is a breed of horses who can only carry 6 st. or so respectably? If racing is to improve the breed of horses, as some assert, let us, by all means, have a higher scale of weight. In steeple-chasing, where they have further to go, generally in deep ground and fences to jump, the minimum weight is 10 st., and 7 lbs. less in the Grand National. A three-year-old goes two miles over hurdles up to his fetlocks in mud with 10 st., but the four-year-old bottom weight in the Summer Handicap must only carry 6 st. Besides, it spoils the temper of horses being ridden by weak boys. They find out their own power over science and the higher animal, man, and once they

do that they take some curing of evil ways.

To further illustrate the fallacy of our present system, two-year-olds in their own races in March, when they are mere babies, carry 8 st. 12 lbs., whilst their older and more matured stable companions are racing with nearly 3 st. less. I should like to see flat-race weights raised 2 st. A voice of horror will soon be raised at this, and will say, "Break them all down;" and a good job if about a third of the useless weeds were broken down, say I. The strongest and best will survive.

What about Cloister, Frigate, the Lamb, the Colonel, Why Not, and hosts of others which stood the test nobly and gallantly for years? These are the sort to do the country good. One hears and reads of owners of classic three-year-olds being called awful names if they ask their glass-case gees to run about five times in a season. "Over-worked," "Pitcher taken to the well once too often," "Temper ruined," and so on; but the poor old Epsom-trained selling-steeplechase plater has to face the music as many times in a fortnight gamely, and get beans, too, for a whole furlong in a "well-timed" finish.

What a lot of the Newmarket trainers have been cross-country riders of note! —Jewitt, Marsh, J. Cannon, Ryan, and C. Archer, for example. I am not sure that Ryan carried silk, but I have seen him go tremendously well with the Newmarket drag and the neighbouring fox and stag hounds.

I knew Mr. Ryan's son, young Jimmy, very well, and it was indeed sad that he should have been "called" so early in life, and with a brilliant career in front of him. He won several local chases on his own horse the season before he died.

Heigho! I'm wandering off to hunting tales again, I see, so must pull up; and that reminds me that I have stuck words on the front page of this "blessed book" as to the way to find winners. Perhaps if I gave the most conscientious and at the same time concise advice possible, it would be a repetition of the words of poor Jimmy Snowden before mentioned. He and Drislane and old Tom Green, the trainers, and two or three more of us, were breakfasting off one of those good solid hot breakfasts for which Yorkshire is famous at the comfortable hostelry at Thirsk, on the second day of the meeting, and a cadaverous-looking man came to the coffee-room and wanted to speak to Mr. Snowden. Jimmy went no more than halfway out of the door, so we could hear what passed; and the stranger, after apologizing for troubling, etc., wanted to know if Jimmy could oblige him with a winner or two, as he had lost nearly all his money, principally through backing Jim's mounts, and he'd a wife and family, and lost his situation, and so on—the old, old story. Yes, Jim thought he could give him a good tip; but had he any money left? Yes, about a couple of sovs. in his pocket. Then said Jimmy, "You darned well keep it there."

After very careful study and consideration, I have come to the conclusion that about five per cent. of the stony brigade, consisting of those who have lost their money and come down in the world, are the victims of bad luck, or are idle and muddlers, and the other ninety-five per cent. can trace the reason of their downfall to one or perhaps more of these three causes, viz. drink, gambling, and excessive gallantry.

Being, as I am, a very-much-married man, with quite a quiverful of noisy boys and girls, and being, moreover, of a retiring and somewhat bashful disposition, I am speaking on this last cause of ruin devoid of any personal experience whatever; but, like a war-horse who sniffs the battle from afar, I have heard of hosts of poor men who have been inveigled and half ruined, and had their peace of mind utterly confused, by coquettish, plotting little bundles of fluff, feathers, silken hose, bewitching smiles, and canary-coloured hair. So, in obedience to candour and truth, I feel impelled to put this all down, and I think that "excessive gallantry" just nicely expresses the weakness of such frail creatures as fall victims to feminine charms and snares.

Over-drinking, undoubtedly, does for a goodly number, but, without wishing to make a saint of myself, there is not very much to confess here. I may have had to scramble to bed odd times by aid of the balustrade and the boots; I may have risen in the morning with a "head," and breakfasted off half a piece of dry toast; but on the whole much harm hasn't followed, and certainly I have no occasion to put this down as one of my besetting sins.

Gambling has done the trick for me, though, and if I, in the certain knowledge that anything I may record will not waver one solitary backer from the error of his ways, still endeavour to point out the most common-sense way in which it should be done, I will not scruple to lay it down as a golden maxim that the pleasure of winning is more than counterbalanced by the misery of losing. Yes, backers of horses play a losing game, because the odds are against them, though it may be, and often is, only slightly. They pursue a fascinating and engrossing phantom at the expense of their business, and are mistrusted by the other half of the community in general and their bankers in particular.

As the moth with blind persistency again and again dips its already scorched wings in the flickering candle-flame, so do we return to the noble pursuit of finding 'em. I can hardly call to mind a solitary example of a man who has once developed this taste ever really relinquishing it. You meet a man in the street and say, " Doing anything to-day, old man ? " " No, I've chucked it for a bit," "Giving it a rest," "Had a good win over the National, and showing 'em the art of gambling;" or, "No, that game's no good to me. I should soon have had to put the shutters up." Wait a while. You'll meet any of these before long either going panting with a sweet smiling face to a meeting, or they'll come and buttonhole you to one side, and tell you in a mysterious whisper they know the biggest cert. they ever knew in all their lives for the Hunt Cup at Ascot. If it runs in a small race at Epsom, don't back it, and don't get stalled off if it runs badly. It's going for the Hunt Cup, and you must get on as soon as ever the betting opens.

If one hasn't been racing for some considerable time—a few months or a season, maybe—it's quite striking to notice all the old familiar faces and a few new ones. Men one knew years ago when we first started the game, some stouter and more prosperous-looking, others diseased and ragged. The man you remember as having seen take 1000 to 80 four times Buchanan for the Lincoln Handicap making a *very* silver book, perhaps, on the outskirts of the silver ring. The man you saw welshing and half bashed to death, as you thought, fifteen years ago at Stockbridge is now betting in Tattersall's ring in thousands over the rails of the members' enclosure, with seven diamond rings on his fingers, and young Koh-i-noors for his shirt-studs. You see a man card-selling whom you knew some years ago as having four horses in training at Lambourne, and you see another who started life turning "cart-wheels" or standing on his head in the street for coppers, then bookmaker's runner, and now owning six or seven horses in one of the crack stables at Newmarket.

There they all are, the racing army; the seasons may come and the seasons may go, favourites get beat and outsiders roll home, they keep on punting bravely still.

I hope none who may read this book will jump to the conclusion that bookmaking is a simple, broad, and easy road to fortune. You can bet unlucky at that game very easily, and go down at it. Then, again, those bookmakers who are at heart backers in disguise, and keep something for the book (that is, not lay it), or back once or twice a day, are not playing their own game properly, and are pretty certain to "come unstuck."

A bookmaker should be a born mathematician, and bet to figures as near as possible, but which is not always practicable, whether you are at the post or betting starting-price away from it. If a man is betting at the post, and there are, for instance, three runners, and they take six to four each of two, the other works out at four to one, but the bookmaker would not be laying more than three to one, which leaves a certain profit, though small. In fields of sixteen runners or so, a bookmaker can often bet or make a round book on about ten or twelve horses, and have the others running for him clear if he has a good connection; and should one of those he has not laid at all roll home, he has a good haul, and can stand a few favourites winning later on.

Bet as you may, however, the book will go wrong when a long sequence of favourites get home. Bookmakers, as a class, are most good-hearted, generous fellows, and always ready to subscribe to any genuine misfortune that may overtake jockeys, officials, or, in fact, any one connected with the turf. There are two or three, unfortunately, that I'm indebted to, and two or three (also unfortunately) that are indebted to me. The worst treatment I've had is having to pay for a bottle now and then. You meet them, and calling up a pal or two with the remark that they've "sprung a bogie," you proceed to the refreshment-bar. I got touched for £400 over one race by an unlucky layer over the Cesarewitch a few seasons ago, but up to now he's not even treated me. I wish times would come good for everybody, then I suppose we should all settle, except the rankest of outsiders. I'm afraid that will hardly happen, though, this side the Millennium.

Who hasn't been welshed, or, having been, will own to it? Their education is as incomplete as those who have not endeavoured to "find the lady" with the three-card men.

I remember I got welshed the very first time I went punting in the small ring, off a very highly respectable and flourishing party doing business as the Pickwick Firm. They were dressed in true Pickwickian costume, and shortly after I met the principal in plain clothes, and, saluting me with a most cordial shake of the hand, expressed his regret that I, of all men, had "tumbled into the net." He stood drinks and cigars, and I am to have my pieces another time ! ! !

The night I got done for £400 at Newmarket off that bookmaker (who was, of course, nothing so common as a welsher, but all the same couldn't pay)

I was standing on the platform at Newmarket Station, and as a train came slowing up, a man jumped off the platform and put his head on the far metal. We had no time to do anything but shudder, and, of course, it was expected he would have to be picked up in basketfuls. However, the protecting-rod in front of the engine-wheel had pushed his head to one side, so he was only scalped, and lived to punt another day. He was in the infirmary for many weeks, and then they tried the poor beggar for attempting suicide. I think they let him off, though, pretty easily. *Moral:* when you want to indulge in these playful jokes, put your neck, not your head, on the metals, or you may only get scalped.

During the recent discussion in the *Daily Telegraph re* the purification of the turf, a lot of rot was written by people who know nothing about it, to the effect that those who won't bet with good bookmakers when there are plenty deserve to lose. How the dickens is a casual attendant at race meetings to distinguish the wheat from the chaff? A punter stands carefully eyeing over a couple of wrong uns, when, sure enough, two "sporting sort of gentlemen" come up at different moments and back something with them to win a pony or so on the Nod. That gives him the necessary confidence, for surely if they are good for that sum they are good for his couple of sovereigns, and into the net he falls.

I think more protection should be given to those who pay their 2s. 6d. or 5s. for entry to the smaller rings at suburban meetings, by having the enclosures kept clearer of wrong uns. It is not because gatekeepers don't know them; it is because managers and clerks of courses, in their anxiety to secure gates resulting in dividends, wink the other eye, and so the game goes on.

Bookmaking is not quite the golden game the uninitiated set it down to be, and few bookmakers amass anything like the fortune ascribed to them, nor do such fortunes bear favourable comparison with those amassed by men in commercial and other walks of life. Of course, the bookmaker lives out of the backer, as does also indirectly the whole racing institution of the country and a good portion of railway profits and the sporting press.

Owners of horses run for very little more money than is subscribed by their own entry and other fees in races cleverly constructed by wily clerks of courses, who get a premium on their own handiwork, and are generally big shareholders in the club meetings as well. You can trace it nearly all directly or indirectly to the merry punter, and of these how many make fortunes, or die better off than when they were born? Not many. A racing man, who knows them all pretty well, can quickly tick them off with his fingers. But the impoverished ones, are they not thick as Vallombrosian leaves throughout the length and breadth of the land? Some flourish like a green bay tree one day, and are stony the next. You've had a good day, you've won £500 to-day, and £300 yesterday, and you know a real good thing for to-morrow, and you've got a two-year-old in training that you ran only half fit in April, when it ran last; it's come on by leaps and bounds, and you'll get it in a nursery in September, bottom weight, and it will be the biggest cert. in all Christendom; and won't you give the bookmakers beans over that cove? Everything is going as merry as the marriage bell, so you dine your friends sumptuously on the very best; do the Empire, and sup at the Savoy, Continental, or friendly Jimmy's—nice life this, when *you know how* to play the game—till a sequence of reverses set in such as have never been heard of before. One cert. ran a deadheat, and got beat in the run off; another got shut in at the critical moment; one twisted a plate when it had the race in hand; a swinging hurdle caught another that couldn't have lost; and the readied two-year-old broke down. Who could stand all this? You take the knock, and instead of betting on the Nod over the rails, you are dashing it down in dollars on the course. I've saved a couple of bobs with Benson, the Jubilee Plunger, within a short time of his betting in tens of thousands. No suppers at St. James's then, you know—just a bun and a cup of cocoa at a penny, and walk up and down the streets to kill time and misery till bedtime.

Some backers of a very even temperament plod on, just living at it for years; but if you want to live at backing horses you must take the money for your guide, and back sometimes three or four in a race to make your money pretty level. I've run guide-books through without end, and studied all systems. There are lots more favourites win than anything else. The fact that when favourites win bookmakers lose speaks for itself. If there is a hot favourite, and the price is six to four on the field before flag-fall, and four, five, or six to one bar one, you should back the favourite; but if there are two favourites at about equal prices, say five to two, or three to one each, and sixes or sevens bar one, back the two favourites, and so on, but there is no set rule, and you *cannot* work it on a system. I've known men with every conceivable system under the sun, and they all come to pieces sooner or later; the book wins. Then it is impossible, when tested by experience, to play your money by increased or curtailed sequences with any chance of success. The sharps and the boys who go racing all the year round are most of them what are called good gamblers—that is, they have pluck or recklessness enough to leave their winnings down (or play them up if you like), and by so doing they occasionally run a few sovereigns into a few hundreds, then they have a good time until they play it down again, and are stony and dependent on their pals for a time. It is this possibility that leads the backer on; it is his bright beacon on the golden shore; but reefers and quicksands intervene sometimes.

Funny lot the racing army are! There's the lumberer—a young fellow dressed quietly and as a gentleman, barring some trifling detail always apparent. He selects his greenhorn, and, biding his time, asks for a light, or, Your pencil a moment. Thanks. Good race; and did you back it? No; did he? Yes; at least, his friend did, who is inside, and knows Watts, or Cannon, or Loates, and does part of their commissions. Indeed? and what might they be going to back for the next race? Ah, he can't tell yet; his friend, even, won't know till the jockeys have arranged it at the last moment, and perhaps then may not be able to bet at all for a couple of races or so lower down the card. Put a tenner on for you? Well, perhaps George might; I'll ask him if you like. They hunt in twos and threes, and George will certainly appear at the right moment. George obliges. Tenner goes down, but there's more to follow; and I've known of hundreds to go in one hand. I knew a case of a clerk in the North who fell a prey till he parted with all he could get hold of, and afterwards drowned himself in the reservoir; but that's only a detail.

The young gentlemen under notice generally work about the coaches at swell meetings, where game is pretty plentiful as a rule. They are unobtrusive, and won't hurt you; take your money, that's all—no vulgarity about them.

Christian friends, would you like to play the lumbering trick just for once? If so, I'll tell you what to do. Just lumber all your friends on to reading the "Merry Gee-Gee." They may never forgive you, perhaps, for playing them such a fiendish joke, but you will have the satisfaction of knowing you have aided in a good cause.

Of tipsters there is no possible doubt but that Old Jack Dickenson is the undoubted champion. Not that I should think it at all likely one tipster gives any more winners than another; in fact, I should say that in a twelvemonth two tipsters would give precisely the same number of winners, or very little difference, just as two people playing at cards together for a week would leave off quits if they played an equally good game. But everybody knows old Jack; he's always there at exercise in a morning on the course, whilst many are not out of bed, and he knows everybody, and is so civil and courteous, and has played the game so unremittingly for years and years. Jack's a dead gambler, or I feel sure he would have been a millionaire; the money he has had off the British public is incredible. He generally owns a few platers when he is flush. The midday editions have knocked the tipsters badly.

The *Roseberry Despatch* was once a flourishing scrip, especially after giving Goldseeker a long-shot City and Suburban winner. I know Mr. Glover, the proprietor, very well, and I saw him looking hale and hearty the other day. He won a thousand-pound nursery at Derby with a two-year-old he called after his paper. Then Mr. Hartley, another tipster, owned several platers a year or so ago.

The whisperer is a bird of different

plumage. He has a goodly number of private country clients on his book, to whom he sends "paddock wires;" and if two horses seem to monopolize a race pretty well between them, he, of course, sends one as a cert. to half his clients, the other half having the other gee as a snip, so he has two strings to his bow, and can't very well crab them all one day: moreover, fresh mugs keep being born as old ones die off. He has his regular saddling paddock punters, too, with whom he can be seen holding serious converse in corners and behind shrubs. What a gullish herd stay-at-home backers are! They don't bet till they get something "sent" from such as these or a discharged stable boy. Do owners keep horses in training at enormous expense to divulge their intentions in these channels? But your backer must have mystery, or he's not "in the know."

My child, my dear, trustful, innocent child, there's not half, nor a tenth part the mystery in it all you imagine, and when there is you won't know until after, and most likely not then. You make no allowance for in and out running. You can't seem to understand that horses are not like machines, so many pounds of steam and a given speed. You know nothing of slips, bad starts, suppressed coughs, bumpings, some other horse come on and another gone off. It is unsavoury to you to think that in the Stewards' Cup of twenty runners everybody connected with quite ten of them are sanguine of success, that is not mysterious enough for you, but it is nevertheless a fact. When the horse you've backed is beat you give expression to a doubt you had entertained that he was not on the job this time, but they're not going to kid you; you mean to wait and back him next time he runs; he must be watched. There is, as a matter of fact, very much less of the "down the course," "stiff un," and "Johnny Armstrong" jockey business than the outside public imagine.

There is plenty in the natural constitution of a horse and the transition from greenness and want of condition to perfection to account for reversal of form and confound handicappers and the public, without attempting to bluff them by vulgar means. Your two-year-old is coming on daily, but not more than half fit yet; but you want his eyes opening in public and using to the rustle of silk, and as he's engaged in the Produce Stakes and you will have the forfeit to pay anyhow, you run him and say to your jockey,

"I'm not backing him to-day, as he is hardly to my liking, but I am anxious to win the Prince of Wales' Nursery next month. He's bound to win that if he runs badly to-day, and gets in at a decent weight, so don't knock him about, it's a pity in his condition, and then you can ride him again in the Prince of Wales' Nursery, when we mean to have a real gamble."

To further illustrate. Your horse lacks the dash for a five-furlong race, but is useful at a mile, and more than useful at a mile and a half, so you persistently run him out of his course in five-furlong events in which he makes no show, till eventually you enter him in a mile-and-a-half race, getting bottom weight, and you have a dash, as you've got a stone in hand; but, woe betide you! there's another gee trained in the North, with two stone up his sleeve, been playing the same game, and you get beaten in a canter by four lengths.

So the noble game is played; but what matter, when you are in the know of a real cop for the Cambridgeshire, which is to be the grand retriever for all your losses of the year, and you mean to back it "till the cows come home"? It overpowers its light-weight boy, and runs three times to the bushes in false starts, but performs respectably in the race, considering what it had taken out of itself before the race, so it must be backed again in a welter race with a man up, and so on.

I've just remembered the case of a man who made an error worth recounting. It was the Alexandra Park meeting, June, 1893, and I was at home, and walking up street in the afternoon, I met my friend, and said, "Good afternoon,

George. Done anything?" "Yes, tenner on that rotten Garland, and just got result wire; he's beat. He's in the last race too, and they may run him again, so I'm going to wire and cry off that. I can't afford to lose £20 over that crock to-day; I've been having a bad time." In the last race there were three runners, with a long odds-on chance favourite; but Garland started at 100 to 8, and won easily, so that second wire lost my friend £125, and George took a three days' booze on the strength of it. Garland belonged to Mr. Savage, a Lewes sportsman, who previously owned Adanapaar, a very well-bred and useful sort of horse, on whom, however, I dropped £300 one day, and his owner four sovereigns.

I won my first bet, I remember so well, when I was at school at Lincoln.

THE NOBLE ART OF BACKING WINNERS 199

I got expelled from two boarding-schools out of three—at least, I got expelled from one, and the mater was politely requested to remove me from another, which was much the same thing. By some manœuvring I managed to get off to the hunt steeplechase meeting just outside the city, and I had 5s. to 4s. Barbarian, a horse belonging to Mr. Sam Welfitt of Tathwell, and ridden by Mr. Rippon Brockton, otherwise known as *old* Rip Brockton, even in those days, thirty years ago. He was judging at a horse show the other day where I was showing, and looks very little older now than he did then. Up to the time he gave up riding, there was no more popular gentleman rider in Nottinghamshire and Lincolnshire of a certainty than Mr. Brockton. I did my winnings in and a bit more to it before I left the course, but, nothing daunted, I've been playing the great game off and on ever since.

After I left school, our grocer was my bookmaker. Sporting grocers are about as rare as non-sporting butchers, and as for a non-sporting barber, he is unworthy his high calling. Do not mighty turf secrets emanate from our friend the sporting barber? Does he not shave a young fellow that courts the cook at the same house where the housemaid lives that Dawson's head travelling-lad is going to marry? or doesn't Bill Cash, the bookmaker, have his hair cut at our friend the tonsorial artist's? Anyhow, our grocer was my bookmaker till I got older and fixed, and knew more, and wanted to dash more down and pick more up; so I played the game more gallantly, and as time went on got to bet in ponies, and fifties, and hundreds with varying success. Of course, I was only in quite a middle-class position of life, so winning or losing two or three thousand a year was playing it fairly for me, though very small potatoes to those who bet on the higher scale.

The man who bets in monkeys (£500) on a race looks with a mild pity on the man who bets in ponies (£25), who also, in his turn, has profound contempt for a man who dabbles in ones and twos. I got a run of luck sometimes—got some long-priced ones home now and then. I had a good autumn when Ossian won the Leger, capturing £700 over him, followed by £1150 over Bendigo for the Cambs., and £1300 Boswell the Liverpool Autumn Cup. I backed this gee at the Lincoln meeting at tens; then he was knocked out, and I had forty to one to a few sovereigns, and went and backed him at the post at, I think, about three to one.

Soon after this I had a big reverse in business, so I went for it back on the turf keener than ever. I had a real bad day in store shortly after this period. I got in the know of the deadest snip that ever was known in a hunters' flat race at Sandown Park. This mare was said to have so much in hand that if she tumbled down she'd have time to get up again and win. I backed it at all sorts of prices down to six to four. Had £1200 on, and stood to win about £3000 over the race. There were eleven runners, and the dead snip finished third. I had every proof afterwards that, as a punishment for taking all the cream of the market, I was put "in the cart" over that job, and next time out that mare won in a canter by six lengths. I dropped £400 more over the next two races, and then took £1600 to £400 on a certain horse in a steeplechase. Mr. George Lambton was on the favourite, a six to four chance, and after it fell, the far side against the railway gates, they shouted ten to one on my gee. There were only two at all in it, mine going strong and well, and the other in distress, so much so, in fact, that his heart misgave him as they neared the last fence, and he swerved right across into mine, and down they both came a cropper; meanwhile one of the rank outsiders came up from behind, and got the race. That swerve cost me £2000, and as I walked over Waterloo Bridge that night I should have taken very little persuading to drown my sorrows in old Father Thames. I had only just entered the grinding mill then, though, but haven't I just been through it again and again since then!

Yes, I climbed down steadily, still a patron of the sport of kings, rubbing shoulders with the scum of the earth, punting bravely in shillings, and sometimes pounds, as fortune wavered.

About this time I used to make a book occasionally with a pal, and I remember on one occasion we stood up in the shilling ring at Manchester with a bank of £20. Favourites rolled home with a cruel persistency the first two days, till we had to face the music with two sovereigns on the Saturday morning.

It was the day Raffaello won the November Handicap, and the course was under water on the far side, and very heavy all over. We laid them as level as we could, and had to back any overlaid ones in with a neighbour each race. They were big fields, and outsiders (which we managed to miss) got home to such a tune that by giving all the money a chance each time we had £57 in the satchell at the day's end. We never had to pay over anything to any extent all day.

Coming up from Warwick to Manchester on this occasion, I remember having a close ride. We scrambled into a third-class carriage of the special from Warwick to Manchester, after racing at the former place; and, of course, we were five a side—cash bookmakers and the usual motley crew. Just as the train was moving off, there came tumbling through the window of the locked off-side door, five riders, or samples of the boys, without tickets, so we were pretty thick—fifteen of us, for an hour and a half's ride. When we slowed up for the ticket exam. place, we stowed the two fattest under each seat, put the thinnest on the hat-rack, and covered with mackintoshes, etc., and the other two laid behind us on the seats, carefully hidden. Our journey was lively enough, as the boys were full of anecdotes, and not at all apprehensive as to what hotel they were going to stop at on arriving at Manchester.

About this time the enclosed coursing meetings were all the rage, and I frequented them a good deal, and have been to Kempton, Plumpton, Four Oaks, Haydock, and Gosforth Park, all of which are now done away with. I have seen five or six Waterloo Cups, and high times we had at the Adelphi, at Liverpool, when things were rosy. Fullerton was a grand greyhound at all points, and no mistake. I have been to most coursing meetings in England and Scotland; the open coursing is far preferable to the enclosed system in my opinion. Coursing is a terrible gamble, almost worse than racing, and public coursing after driven hares is about as far removed from riding after a brace of greyhounds on your own farm, as the battue from shooting over a brace of well-broken pointers, and walking to your own game.

One day, in those times of rampant impecuniosity, I had a stroke of luck. I was engaged in the *lofty* pursuit of driving a hansom and making a tiny S.P. book amongst my pal cabbies, and a gentleman hailed me one night to take to a certain address two real ladies, both of whom had been taking a wee drop more than was good for them. The gentleman rode in the cab too, and what a job we had unloading them! They got their legs through the spokes of the wheels, and rolled under the horse, which, luckily, was very quiet, as cab-horses *sometimes* are ; but eventually, with the aid of a passing navvy, we dragged them inside. The sportsman gave me a sovereign, and told me to put it on Tib for the Stewards' Cup, which I did, and it won at twenty-five to one. It was partly as hush-money, too, I think, as the place was not very big, and he was a town councillor, or something of that sort. I kept my trust pretty well, too, as I've never breathed a word from that day to this, and even now I have not divulged the name of the town, have I?

Often in those days, when I had nothing to do, no money, and no means of earning any, I used to have a day's hunting on foot; and I have walked and run miles and miles a day after the hounds. If ever I'd captured a loose horse, you bet I'd have had a good ride; but none such ever happened to cross my path. From having dropped to poverty, misery, and despair, I managed, through bringing my auctioneering abilities into play, to creep back into a moderately decent position of £500 a year; but, still saturated with confidence in my knowledge of the Turf, and having, as I thought, a nose for winners—which however, often have a beastly habit of running second only—I find myself somewhat (and a very big somewhat, too) stranded once more on the pebbly beach, and lowered to the utter degradation of writing this jumble.

Having touched on jockeys and betting, surely I ought to say something of the gees themselves. Accordingly, I may as well say, without further parley, that Ormonde is my "best horse." I saw him run all his races, I think; and give me a horse good at all distances, and that was never beaten. Not only that, but in dealing with Ormonde we must remember he reigned in a season rich in good horses, several of which would have made a rare example of most of our classic performers this season.

The two most interesting races I have seen were the Two Thousand Guineas Ormonde won, and the Hardwicke Stakes at Ascot, wherein he beat Minting and Bendigo. Minting was considered by Matt Dawson an extraordinary horse, and so he was, indeed, and when, after having backed him for the Two Thousand Guineas, I stood and saw the easy way in which Ormonde strode away from him out of the Abingdon Mile bottom, I said to myself, "What manner of horse is this I see?" Saraband and St. Mirin were behind the two, and he served the sturdy and speedy little Bard the same way in the Derby.

I remember a tremendous performance of his in one of the numerous Newmarket biennials, in which he gave stones to the very speedy Mephisto over five furlongs, and left him standing still.

Doubtless, at Ascot, when Minting made a race of it with him, and with Bendigo close up, his wind infirmity was beginning to tell upon him. In Ormonde, Archer, and John Porter one got rather a useful trio—horse, jockey, and trainer; and verily they took some beating.

Without a doubt Bendigo and Victor Wild have been the two most popular handicap horses of modern times, and the former is a striking example of a great racehorse proving a great stud failure, and I hope Victor Wild will do better.

Bendigo would have won the Cambridgeshire the year Gloriation was first, right enough, if Johnny Osborne had come sooner. I was standing on the top ground just where his jockey asked him the question, and he shot out like a bullet, but it was too late. People said unkind things of Osborne because he trained the winner, but he's as honest as the day—simply committed an error of judgment, that's all. Bendigo wanted the *great little* Tod up. I place Bendigo as the greatest handicap horse I have known, as, although Minting was undeniable at medium distances, I question his ability to have got the Cesarewitch course as Bendigo did; and I class the latter's performance, when he ran second to Humewood, conceding stones, as quite one of the best on record, independent of his winning record as a miler. If

I remember right, Bendigo carried 9 st. 10 lbs., and was giving about a stone to a horse like Carlton, a proved high-class stayer, and several other good ones, whom he beat any distance. Yes, undoubtedly this was a very great performance. Speaking of Carlton and of horses running in all shapes, did anybody ever see a horse look so little like the veritable stayer he undoubtedly was? High, narrow, and split up behind in a most marked degree. Still, handsome is as handsome does, as the saying goes; and Carlton's performances speak for themselves.

The fact of so many examples brought to our notice, and doubly emphasized of late, of unfashionably bred horses beating their more fashionable rivals, should lend encouragement to small owners to buy low-priced yearlings, so long as they stick to size and good formation, independent of their being bred to figures; and I strongly recommend this course to large farmers or such as have plenty of land accommodation, and grow their own corn and forage on a cheap scale. Break your own yearlings, and get them ship-shape and about half fit. You will soon see if there is anything worth sending to train, and the others can lay by for hunters and chasers later on in life.

We have had many striking illustrations of selling-platers showing marked improvement under different management, notably Victor Wild, and quite recently Chalereux and Herminius. Change of stables and different training and a man understanding his business bring this about; one horse thrives only on a mild preparation, whilst another glutton can't have too much work;

and one great cause of bad doing is their teeth.

I know a celebrated equine dentist whose labours have produced wonderful results through extracting diseased and filing down sharp projecting teeth. I have seen horses with their gums all boils and sores through sharp teeth continually rubbing against them, and have known such horses develop irritability, and their attendants unable to attribute the cause, and have seen them, after a few minutes' treatment by the man I refer to, rub their noses on his arms, and almost lick his hands in gratitude.

I remember buying a two-year-old some years ago for a little money after running last in a race. His gums had a rancorous incision in which you could have laid your finger, caused by his teeth. In a few weeks after dentistry he came on beyond recognition. It so happened I had a very bad Ascot just then, losing £500, which was a good lot for me at that particular time, so I entered the colt in an overnight selling at Alexandra Park on the Saturday, and wired for him to be sent on. I had a fair splash on him, backing him more particularly for a place. I told my jockey he was an idle horse, wanting a lot of riding, and told him to keep plugging it into him all the way. Passing the post a sheet would have covered the first four, and mine, coming as one dropped from the clouds, got beat out of place by no more than the length of your hand. He was catching them every stride, and would have won outright in two or three more lengths. My jockey had not started riding him soon enough. I wish I had Tod Sloan up; he'd have won, right enough.

He won next time out easily, and the next also, and I did very well, getting over £400 out of him.

Another matter which tends to upset form is the fact that plenty of horses who can act on the hard ground are helpless in the mud, and *vice versâ;* and whilst some can act on give-and-take courses like Epsom and Brighton, others can't get downhill, owing to faulty shoulder placement. Leicester is a funny course—switchback-railway sort of business, and quite a pitfall for backers. If a horse performs well there once, he will generally do the same again. Rusticus, who captured two very rich handicaps there, but could not win elsewhere for love or money, was a striking illustration of this.

I give steeplechasing a decided preference over flat-racing from a sporting point of view, though it is more risky gambling, and I question if I have ever seen one to beat Cloister at the game; but there is so much difference between a chaser who can just get two miles brilliantly and one who can with safety negotiate and stay at full speed the Grand National course, that comparisons (without being odious) are difficult to make and of small account. Although Cloister by no means filled the eye as the stayer and weight-carrier he was, being not over-well ribbed up, and with a moderate back and rather split up, a more brilliant performance could not be imagined than the way in which he cut up his Liverpool field, carrying the biggest weight on record, making the whole of the running, and winning by forty lengths. That was a capital illustration of what I advocated further back as to letting top weights stride along, thus giving them an opportunity to bring their merits into play. Cloister skimmed his fences like a swallow, and you hardly saw him jump at all—he seemed to gallop over them, as perfect chasers should.

Slow horses often win chases through their perfect fencing, but not as often as of yore. They are mostly speedy recruits from the flat; and a very fast hunter, if not quite thoroughbred and well schooled, has no earthly chance against selling steeplechasers, who, besides having some pace about them, are so used to jumping at full speed that they lose no time at their fences. I do not take exception to the guard-rail fence to the extent many do, as I have trained plenty who will go and jump it right enough the very first time they are asked. When you start an ordinary hunter chasing, it is the increased pace at which he is asked to jump that confuses him. Stallions intended for being transferred from the flat to steeplechasing are far better added to the list, and so would be a good many flat-racers I know of. Joe Cannon is one trainer I can mention as a disciple of this doctrine. Nearly all the sons and grandsons of Hermit show a natural adaptability to jump and sire jumpers of note. Natural jumpers are generally placid-tempered horses, and minus the excitability of the St. Simons, for instance.

Nothing can possibly be more irritating to young thoroughbreds than our system of starting; and, with great deference to the ability of Mr. Arthur Coventry, I, for one, am a great believer in the starting-gate, and hope it will be universal here shortly. Surely the new rules of the Jockey Club promoting long-distance racing must have a beneficial effect in fostering chasers by encouraging a stouter breed, and at the same time a breed of more service to the country. A wretched-looking, weedy two-year-old well forward may be a source of remuneration for early two-year-old racing, but they are no good for Grand National horses or anything else later in life.

It is puzzling to account for the fact that speedy five-furlong horses who could not stay at all on the flat often prove brilliant hurdle-racers, and can with ease stay two miles at that game, whilst horses that could have given them stones at two miles on the flat can't hold a candle to them over hurdles. I attribute the reason to smart jumping and quickness in getting on their legs again. Bonnie Lassie was the quickest mare I ever saw over hurdles, and could not get more than five furlongs on the flat. Without glasses you could not detect her jump at all a short distance off; her effort was so even and slight as to be imperceptible.

There's real and genuine pleasure in the local hunt-race meetings all over the country, where one knows each horse and each rider, and the ladies want all the winners finding and their fortunes telling; luncheons, minstrelsy, the popping of champagne-corks, and all the paraphernalia. I should rather like to see some new rule passed enabling genuine hunters to have a chance in hunters' flat races, as used to prevail, but which under the present system are entirely devoted to race-horses, and in which a Quorn or Belvoir hunter would have no chance. There's a private sweepstake at Croxton Park every year of this nature which is most popular, and always commands no end of runners. Croxton Park meeting must be one of the oldest in the country, and very popular with all the country side—everybody goes for miles round ; and that reminds me what tricks people have to get off for a day's racing who do not wish their sedate neighbours to know they follow such an evil pursuit.

I have in my mind's eye a very highly respectable solicitor, quite a model of propriety, etc., but he does love finding 'em, and I often go and discuss with him the chances of prominent candidates for future events. When this hardened old sinner is off out for a day's racing, he carries a legal-looking black bag with him, and a bundle of blue papers tied with pink tape. These he takes with him to the first junction on the line, and there they are carefully deposited in the parcels-office, to be brought out again for a cloak to the inquisitive on his return from having been "up to town to *consult his London agent.*" Mighty fond of poker he is; nearly all racing men are fond of cards and billiards.

I can't say these two mediums have cost me anything. I've certainly played cards when we've won or lost £400 or £500 a sitting, but I don't think they owe me anything. If a man has the bump of speculation, it's very hard to go against it. I'm quite a believer in phrenology. It requires a lot of determination to go against your bumps; and fighting against idleness, want of punctuality, over-extravagance, etc., must be a greater virtue in the man who has those undesirable bumps, and consequently inclinations, than it is in the man who has the reverse bumps and the reverse inclinations.

The Salvation Army have no occasion to wear a uniform—they carry it all in their faces, with few exceptions; your anarchist has it in his phiz; and for further evidence take a walk round the Chamber of Horrors at Madame Tussaud's.

It's rather funny how persistent backers of horses have their lucky and unlucky meetings, and bet a little extra or a little careful as the case may be; they are a very superstitious class, too, as a rule. York, Liverpool, and the old Croydon meetings were my lucky ones, and Ascot —oh, dreadful Ascot!—my unlucky one.

I can't imagine the reason, but I always seemed in for some fun and enjoyment the minute I set foot in York. It's always sure to develop sooner or later from some unforeseen source. I remember one great night years ago. We had had a real good time, backed all the winners, and so on, and dined wisely and well at the Station Hotel, where we stayed, spending the evening in the usual convivial way—big cigars and the finest brands of wine or liquor, as the case might be. We strolled outside just before midnight to have a cooler, and there espied a big four-wheel Post Office dray, waiting for the midnight mails. "Who'd like a drive?" somebody said. In a twinkling we were all up, me postillion, riding the horse, and my legs hanging over the shafts. My word! the stones rattled and the policemen's whistles blew as we galloped full tilt all round York city, and kept on holloaing imaginary hounds out of cover. We left the dray somewhere after a while, and skedaddled, to escape being locked up, as we deserved. The Post Office officials found their dray again somehow, as I've often seen it outside York Station since, and always doff my hat. I paid the penalty by having the skin scraped off the inside of my legs with those blessed shafts.

What splendid ideas of good living Yorkshire people have, with hot cakes for breakfast quite an institution; and how the racing man relishes, as the seasons recur, the different specialties—Dee salmon at Chester, Sausages at Newmarket, Northampton pork pies, grouse at York (August), Doncaster butterscotch, Pontefract cakes, and so on!

Every one is, I should imagine, disappointed the first time they go to Newmarket; the contrast is so great to Sandown, Kempton, and other club meetings, with their military bands, flowers, and drawing-room sort of entertainment. They consider the finishing at different posts absurd, and the journey to the Cambs. course at top of the town a farce. But Newmarket improves on acquaintance, as one knows it better; it is all the real business side of racing here, and endurance of the place soon gives way to real fondness and appreciation as you become accustomed to the different courses with their different gradients, and a lover of the thoroughbred has countless opportunities for taking note at morning work on the Limekilns or Bury Hills, and in Messrs. Tattersall's sale paddock. It needs an abler pen than mine to describe the glories of Ascot, or the picturesque charms of Goodwood; but for real business commend me to Newmarket, where the very air smells of racing, so to speak—and a peculiarly bracing air it is, too, having a sweet scent peculiarly its own on a Two Thousand Guineas morning in April. Your average racing man needs a fair constitution to stand the exposure and travelling in wet things one often has to endure.

Everybody has heard of Hackness' Cambs. day, or rather the day on which it was postponed owing to the storm, and of Robert the Devil's Leger, when a boat would have floated comfortably in the paddock, on both of which occasions I was present; but for swallowing pure oxygen and catching all the winds that blow, commend me to Lewes downs or Cannock Chase, where once at a coursing meeting we experienced the worst tornado I ever was in.

What charming training-quarters one sees at Newmarket, and dotted about all over the country! There is, however, no prettier or more cosy little spot anywhere than Tom Cannon's little castle at Danebury, the scene of so many grand coups in the high gambling Hastings era. Tom Cannon lays his grounds out in flowers of his own racing colours, red and white stripes, and each time he has had a son or daughter born, he places a miniature wooden cannon on top of an embankment in the garden. I sometimes think, if I had fifteen Maxims judiciously placed round our little chateau, I could keep a whole army of writters and bums, and such like invaders, at bay for ever so long, and one could have rare fun.

Gentlest, most patient of readers, my race is run, my sun is set, so far as this book is concerned, and solemnly do I swear and promise never to write another. It is now just ten days since I "took one" off my brake, and my contusions and bruises being sufficiently recovered to allow of me once more mixing with my fellow-men, I do so with very mixed feelings. Firstly, have I not registered that copper-bottomed vow (never to be broken) which shall secure me from backing any more losers?

and, secondly, my brain has become so muddled through hatching this ditty, that the wonder is I am not stark staring mad. I am deeply conscious of the fact that I have now left unsaid many things that I ought to have said, and that I have said things which I perhaps ought not to have said—that I have, in short, made a very big fool of myself (but it won't be the first time, or the last, either, I'm afraid); and I suppose the only solatium to such a one as I is that others may take warning: and whilst I have just enough courage to hope that some of my observations regarding breeding of horses may not be entirely barren of good fruit; that my chapters on riding and breaking may impress on some recruit the necessity of loosing their horses' heads at the right moment; that I have portrayed the hunting of the little red rover as the noblest and least demoralizing sport old England boasts; I also know, without any possible shadow of doubt whatever, that nothing I have said will deter brave punters from bravely punting on and on; yet if, in laying bare my varied experiences, I prevent a few such persevering spirits from "falling into the net," getting "lumbered," or wasting their spare cash on "paddock finals;" and, furthermore, should this "sportsman's autobiography" dissemble a newly born idea in a fluttering breast that the backer's couch is a bed of roses, and his path strewn with gold for the mere picking up, may not a wee moral have been taught, and a useful lesson learned, from the perusal of the "Merry Gee-Gee"?

PRINTED BY WILLIAM CLOWES AND SONS, LIMITED,
LONDON AND BECCLES.

F. V. WHITE & CO.'S
Catalogue of Publications

ALEXANDER (Mrs.).
Barbara, Lady's Maid and Peeress. 6s.
The Cost of Her Pride. 6s.
Mrs. Crichton's Creditor. 2s. 6d.
A Golden Autumn. 2s. 6d. and 2s.
A Fight with Fate. 2s. 6d. and 2s.

ATLEE (H. FALCONER).
The Seasons of a Life. 6s.
A Woman of Impulse. 6s.

ALLEN (GRANT).
A Splendid Sin. 3s. 6d. and 2s.

ARMSTRONG (Mrs.).
Letters to a Bride. 2s. 6d. | Good Form. 2s., cloth.

BOUSTEAD (LEILA).
The Blue Diamonds. 1s. and 1s. 6d.

BENTLEY (H. CUMBERLAND).
A Near Thing. 1s.

CAMERON (Mrs. LOVETT).
A Man's Undoing. 6s. and 2s. 6d. | The Ways of a Widow. 6s.
Two Cousins and a Castle. 3s. 6d. | A Sister's Sin. 2s. 6d. and 2s.
Little Lady Lee. 2s. 6d. and 2s. | Weak Woman. 2s. 6d. and 2s.
A Soul Astray. 2s. 6d. and 2s. | A Daughter's Heart. 2s. 6d. and 2s.
A Tragic Blunder. 2s. 6d. and 2s. | A Lost Wife. 2s. 6d. and 2s.
A Bachelor's Bridal. 2s. 6d. and 2s. | In a Grass Country. 1s. and 3s. 6d.
| The Man Who Didn't. 1s. and 1s. 6d.

CLEEVE (LUCAS).
The Monks of the Holy Tear. 6s.

CROMMELIN (MAY).
The Freaks of Lady Fortune. 2s. 6d. and 2s.

CROMMELIN (MAY) and BROWN (J. MORAY).
Violet Vyvian, M.F.H. 2s. 6d. and 2s.

14, BEDFORD STREET, STRAND, W.C.

R

F. V. WHITE & CO., PUBLISHERS

CALMOUR (ALFRED).
The Confessions of a Door Mat. 1s. and 1s. 6d.

DAY (WILLIAM).
Turf Celebrities I Have Known. 16s.

FENN (GEORGE MANVILLE).
Cursed By a Fortune. 6s. and 2s., cloth.
The Case of Ailsa Gray. 3s. 6d. and 2s.

FARJEON (B. L.)
Miriam Rozella. 6s.
The March of Fate. 2s. 6d. and 2s.
Basil and Annette. 2s. 6d. and 2s.
A Young Girl's Life. 2s. 6d. and 2s.
Toilers of Babylon. 2s. 6d. and 2s.

FRASER (Mrs. ALEXANDER).
A Modern Bridegroom. 2s.

FETHERSTONHAUGH (The Honourable Mrs.).
Dream Faces. 2s. 6d.

GRIFFITH (GEORGE).
The Destined Maid. 6s.
Knights of the White Rose. (Illustrated.) 3s. 6d.
Romance of Golden Star. (Illustrated.) 3s. 6d. and 2s.
The Gold Finder. (With Frontispiece.) 3s. 6d.

GROSSMITH (WEEDON).
A Woman with a History. 1s. and 1s. 6d.

GORDON (LORD GRANVILLE).
The Race of To-Day. 6s. | Warned Off. 6s.

GRIMWOOD (Mrs. FRANK ST. CLAIR).
The Power of an Eye. 1s. and 1s. 6d.

GOWING (Mrs. AYLMER).
Gods of Gold. 6s.
Merely Players. 6s.

HENTY (G. A.)
A Woman of the Commune. A Tale of Two Sieges of Paris. (Illustrated.) 6s. and 3s. 6d.

HUNGERFORD (Mrs.).
The Coming of Chloe. 6s. and 2s. 6d.

14, BEDFORD STREET, STRAND, W.C.

HUMBERT (MABEL).
Continental Chit Chat. 1s.

HUME (FERGUS).
The Man with a Secret. 2s. 6d. and 2s.
The Gentleman Who Vanished. 1s. and 1s. 6d.
Miss Mephistopheles. 1s.

HUMPHRY (Mrs.) ("MADGE," of *Truth*).
Housekeeping. 3s. 6d.

JOCELYN (Mrs. ROBERT).
Miss Rayburn's Diamonds. 6s.
Lady Mary's Experiences. 2s. 6d.
Only a Flirt. 2s. 6d.
For One Season Only. A Sporting Novel. 2s. 6d. and 2s.
A Regular Fraud. 2s. 6d. and 2s.
Only a Horse-Dealer. 2s. 6d. and 2s.
A Big Stake. 2s. 6d. and 2s.
Drawn Blank. 2s. 6d. and 2s.
The Criton Hunt Mystery. 2s. 6d. and 2s.
The M.F.H.'s Daughter. 2s. 6d. and 2s.

KENNARD (Mrs. EDWARD).
At the Tail of the Hounds. 2s. 6d.
A Riverside Romance. 2s. 6d. & 2s.
Fooled by a Woman. 2s. 6d.
The Plaything of an Hour, and Other Stories. 2s. 6d. and 2s.
The Catch of The County. 2s. 6d. and 2s.
Wedded To Sport. 3s. 6d. and 2s.
The Hunting Girl. 2s. 6d. and 2s.
Just Like a Woman. 2s. 6d. and 2s.
Sporting Tales. 2s. 6d. and 2s.
Twilight Tales. (Illustrated.) 2s. 6d.
That Pretty Little Horse-breaker. 2s. 6d. and 2s.
Straight as a Die. 2s. 6d. and 2s.
Matron or Maid. 2s. and 2s. 6d.
A Crack County. 2s. 6d. and 2s.
Landing a Prize. 2s. 6d. and 2s.
A Homburg Beauty. 2s. 6d. and 2s.
Our Friends in The Hunting Field. 2s. 6d. and 2s.
The Mystery of a Woman's Heart. 1s. and 1s. 6d.
The Sorrows of a Golfer's Wife. 2s.
A Guide Book for Lady Cyclists. 1s. and 1s. 6d.
The Girl in the Brown Habit. 3s. 6d. (Illustrated.)

LE QUEUX (WILLIAM).
If Sinners Entice Thee. 6s.
Scribes and Pharisees. 6s.
The Great War in England in 1897. (Illustrated.) 3s. 6d.
Zoraida. (Illustrated.) 3s. 6d.
The Eye of Istar. (Illustrated.) 3s. 6d.
Whoso Findeth a Wife. 6s. and 3s. 6d.
Devil's Dice. 3s. 6d. and 2s.
A Madonna of the Music Halls. 1s. and 1s. 6d.

14, BEDFORD STREET, STRAND, W.C.

LITTLE (Mrs. ARCHIBALD).
A Marriage in China. 6s.

MITFORD (BERTRAM).
The Induna's Wife. (Illustrated.) 3s. 6d.
The Ruby Sword. (Illustrated.) 3s. 6d.

MEADE (Mrs. L. T.).
The Siren. 6s.
Bad Little Hannah. (Illustrated.) 3s. 6d.
A Son of Ishmael. 2s., cloth.
The Way of a Woman. 2s. 6d.

MIDDLEMASS (JEAN).
Blanche Coningham's Surrender. 6s.

MARSH (RICHARD).
The House of Mystery. 6s.

McMILLAN (Mrs. ALEC).
The Evolution of Daphne. 6s.

MATHERS (HELEN).
A Man of To-Day. 2s. 6d. and 2s.

MACGREGOR (Surgeon-Major).
Through the Buffer State; a Record of Recent Travels through Borneo, Siam, and Cambodia. With Ten whole-page Illustrations and a Map. 6s.

MURRAY (DAVID CHRISTIE).
The Investigations of John Pym. 1s. and 1s. 6d.

NISBET (HUME).
For Liberty. 3s. 6d.
A Sweet Sinner. 3s. 6d. and 2s.
The Rebel Chief. 3s. 6d. and 2s.
A Desert Bride. 3s. 6d. and 2s.
A Bushgirl's Romance. 3s. 6d. & 2s.

Hunting for Gold. (Illustrated.) 3s. 6d.
The Queen's Desire. 3s. 6d. and 2s.
The Great Secret. 2s. 6d. and 2s.
The Haunted Station. 2s. 6d.
My Love Noel. 2s. 6d. and 2s.

PRAED (Mrs. CAMPBELL).
The Romance of a Châlet. 2s. 6d. and 2s.

PHILIPS (F. C.).
The Luckiest of Three. 1s. and 1s. 6d. | A Devil in Nun's Veiling. 1s. & 1s. 6d.

PHILIPS (F. C.) and PERCY FENDALL.
My Face is My Fortune. 2s. 6d. & 2s. | A Daughter's Sacrifice. 2s. 6d. & 2s.
Margaret Byng. 2s. 6d.

PHILIPS (F. C.) and C. J. WILLS.
Sybil Ross's Marriage. 2s. 6d. and 2s.

"RITA."
Vignettes. 2s. 6d. and 2s.
Joan & Mrs. Carr. 2s. 6d. and 2s.
The Man in Possession. 2s. 6d. & 2s.

The Countess Pharamond. 2s. 6d.
Miss Kate. 2s. 6d. and 2s.

RIDDLE (Mrs.).
A Rich Man's Daughter. 2s. 6d.

ROGERS (C. V.).
Her Marriage Vow. 6s.

ROBERTS (MORLEY).
The Courage of Pauline. 1s. and 1s. 6d.

SIMS (G. R.).
As it Was in the Beginning. 2s. 6d. | The Coachman's Club. 2s. 6d. & 2s.
Dorcas Dene, Detective. 1s. and 1s. 6d., cloth.
Dorcas Dene, Detective. (Second Series.) 1s. and 1s. 6d.

ST. AUBYN (ALAN).
A Fair Impostor. 6s.
A Proctor's Wooing. 6s. & 2s., cloth.
To Step Aside is Human. 2s. 6d. and 2s.

The Wooing of May. 3s. 6d. and 2s.
A Tragic Honeymoon. 2s.
In the Sweet West Country. 2s. 6d. and 2s.

STUART (ESMÈ).
Arrested. 6s. | The Strength of Two. 6s.

SERGEANT (ADELINE).
Told in the Twilight. 2s. 6d. and 2s.
In Vallombrosa. 3s. 6d.

A Valuable Life. 6s.

THOMAS (ANNIE).
Four Women in the Case. 6s. | Essentially Human. 6s.

WARDEN (FLORENCE).
Girls will be Girls. 6s.
Dolly the Romp. (Illustrated.) 3s. 6d.
Our Widow. 2s. 6d. and 2s.
A Lady in Black. 2s. 6d. and 2s.
Dr. Darch's Wife. 2s. 6d. and 2s.
A Spoilt Girl. 2s. 6d. and 2s.
A Perfect Fool. 2s. 6d. and 2s.
Strictly Incog. 2s. 6d. and 2s.
My Child and I. 2s. 6d. and 2s.
A Wild Wooing. 2s. 6d. and 2s.
The Girls at the Grange. 2s. 6d.

Little Miss Prim. 6s.
The Mystery of Dudley Horne. 2s. 6d.
A Young Wife's Trial. 2s. 6d. & 2s.
Kitty's Engagement. 2s. 6d. & 2s.
A Woman's Face. 2s.
The Woman with the Diamonds. 1s. and 1s. 6d.
A Scarborough Romance. 1s. and 1s. 6d.
Two Lads and a Lass. 1s. & 1s. 6d.

WINTER (JOHN STRANGE).

The Price of a Wife. 3s. 6d.
The Peacemakers. 6s.
Everybody's Favourite. 3s. 6d.
Into an Unknown World. 2s. 6d.
The Strange Story of My Life. 2s. 6d. and 2s.
Truth Tellers. 2s. 6d.
A Magnificent Young Man. 2s. 6d. and 2s.
A Blameless Woman. 2s. 6d. and 2s.
A Born Soldier. 2s. 6d. and 2s.
A Seventh Child. 2s. 6d. and 2s.
The Soul of the Bishop. 2s. 6d. and 2s.
Aunt Johnnie. 2s. 6d. and 2s.
My Geoff. 2s. 6d. and 2s.
The Same Thing with a Difference. 1s. and 1s. 6d.
I Married a Wife. (Profusely Illustrated.) 1s. and 1s. 6d.
Private Tinker; and other Stories. (Profusely Illustrated.) 1s. and 1s. 6d.
The Major's Favourite. 1s. & 1s. 6d.
The Stranger Woman. 1s. & 1s. 6d.
Red Coats. (Profusely Illustrated.) 1s. and 1s. 6d.
A Man's Man. 1s. and 1s. 6d.
That Mrs. Smith. 1s. and 1s. 6d.
Three Girls. 1s. and 1s. 6d.
Mere Luck. 1s. and 1s. 6d.
Lumley the Painter. 1s. & 1s. 6d.
Good-Bye. 1s. and 1s. 6d.
Heart and Sword. 6s.

Only Human. 2s. 6d. and 2s.
The Other Man's Wife. 2s. 6d. and 2s.
Army Society. 2s.
A Siege Baby. 2s. 6d. and 2s.
Beautiful Jim. 2s. 6d. and 2s.
Garrison Gossip. 2s. 6d. and 2s.
Mrs. Bob. 2s. 6d. and 2s.
Two Husbands. 1s. and 1s. 6d.
A Gay Little Woman. 1s. and 1s. 6d.
A Seaside Flirt. 1s. and 1s. 6d.
The Troubles of an Unlucky Boy. 1s. and 1s. 6d.
Grip. 1s. and 1s. 6d.
I Loved her Once. 1s. and 1s. 6d.
He Went for a Soldier. 1s. and 1s. 6d.
Ferrers Court. 1s. and 1s. 6d.
A Little Fool. 1s. and 1s. 6d.
Buttons. 1s. and 1s. 6d.
Bootles' Children. (Illustrated.) 1s. and 1s. 6d.
The Confessions of a Publisher. 1s. and 1s. 6d.
My Poor Dick. (Illustrated.) 1s. and 1s. 6d.
That Imp. 1s. and 1s. 6d.
Mignon's Secret. 1s. and 1s. 6d.
Mignon's Husband. 1s. and 1s. 6d.
On March. 1s. and 1s. 6d.
In Quarters. 1s. and 1s. 6d.
In the Same Regiment. 1s. and 1s. 6d.

WILLIAMS (W. PHILLPOTTS).
Over the Open. 6s.

YOLLAND (E.).
In Days of Strife. 6s. | Mistress Bridget. 6s.

14, BEDFORD STREET, STRAND, W.C.

F. V. WHITE & CO., PUBLISHERS

SIX SHILLING NOVELS.

In One Vol., Cloth Gilt, Price 6s. each.

HEART AND SWORD. By JOHN STRANGE WINTER.
IF SINNERS ENTICE THEE. By WILLIAM LE QUEUX.
THE COST OF HER PRIDE. By Mrs. ALEXANDER.
THE DESTINED MAID. By GEORGE GRIFFITH.
THE WAYS OF A WIDOW. By Mrs. LOVETT CAMERON.
THE PEACEMAKERS. By JOHN STRANGE WINTER.
MISS RAYBURN'S DIAMONDS. By The Hon. Mrs. JOCELYN.
HER MARRIAGE VOW. By C. V. ROGERS.
A WOMAN OF IMPULSE. By H. FALCONER ATLEE.
SCRIBES AND PHARISEES: A Story of Literary London. By WILLIAM LE QUEUX.
THE MONKS OF THE HOLY TEAR. By LUCAS CLEEVE, Author of "Lazarus," &c.
WARNED OFF. By LORD GRANVILLE GORDON.
THE SIREN. By L. T. MEADE.
THE HOUSE OF MYSTERY. By RICHARD MARSH, Author of "The Beetle."
THE SEASONS OF A LIFE. By H. FALCONER ATLEE.
BLANCHE CONINGHAM'S SURRENDER. By JEAN MIDDLEMASS.
THE STRENGTH OF TWO. By ESMÈ STUART.
MIRIAM ROZELLA. By B. L. FARJEON.
MERELY PLAYERS. By Mrs. AYLMER GOWING.
WHOSO FINDETH A WIFE. By WILLIAM LE QUEUX.
THE RACE OF TO-DAY. By LORD GRANVILLE GORDON.
OVER THE OPEN. By W. PHILLPOTTS WILLIAMS.
A FAIR IMPOSTOR. By ALAN ST. AUBYN.
GIRLS WILL BE GIRLS. By FLORENCE WARDEN.
THE EYE OF ISTAR. By WILLIAM LE QUEUX. (Illustrated.)
THE EVOLUTION OF DAPHNE. By Mrs. ALEC MCMILLAN.
GODS OF GOLD. By Mrs. AYLMER GOWING.
MISTRESS BRIDGET. By E. YOLLAND.
LITTLE MISS PRIM. By FLORENCE WARDEN.

14, BEDFORD STREET, STRAND, W.C.

F. V. White & Co.'s New Series of Gift Books
SUITABLE FOR PRESENTS, SCHOOL PRIZES, &c.

Contains the following list of volumes written by the most popular Authors, and profusely illustrated by eminent Artists.

Crown 8vo, splendidly illustrated, Cloth Covers, price 3s. 6d. each.

KNIGHTS OF THE WHITE ROSE.
By GEORGE GRIFFITH.
Author of
"The Angel of the Revolution."
Illustrated by Hal Hurst.

BAD LITTLE HANNAH.
By MRS. L. T. MEADE.
Illustrated by Gordon Browne.

HUNTING FOR GOLD.
Adventures in Klondyke.
By HUME NISBET.
Illustrated by Hal Hurst.

A WOMAN OF THE COMMUNE.
By G. A. HENTY.
Illustrated by Hal Hurst.

DOLLY THE ROMP.
By FLORENCE WARDEN.
Illustrated by F. Vigers.

SAPPERS AND MINERS,
By GEORGE MANVILLE FENN.
Illustrated by Hal Hurst.

TRAVELS BY THE FIRESIDE.
By GORDON STABLES, R.N.
Illustrated by Gordon Browne.

A LITTLE MOTHER TO THE OTHERS.
By MRS. L. T. MEADE.
Illustrated by the late Fred Barnard.

CROWN AND ANCHOR.
By J. C. HUTCHESON.
Illustrated by J. B. Greene.

KINGS OF THE SEA.
By HUME NISBET.
Illustrated by J. B. Greene.

THOSE CHILDREN.
By CURTIS YORKE.
Illustrated by Hal Hurst.

THE PIRATE JUNK.
By J. C. HUTCHESON.
Illustrated by J. B. Greene.

THE GREAT WHITE QUEEN.
By WILLIAM LE QUEUX.
Illustrated by A. Pearse.

14, BEDFORD STREET, STRAND, W.C.

F. V. WHITE & CO., PUBLISHERS

Novels at Three Shillings and Sixpence.
In 1 Vol., Cloth Gilt, Price 3s. 6d. each.

The Price of a Wife. By JOHN STRANGE WINTER.
The Ruby Sword. By BERTRAM MITFORD. (Illustrated.)
Whoso Findeth a Wife. By W. LE QUEUX.
The Induna's Wife. By BERTRAM MITFORD. (Illustrated.)
The Gold Finder. By GEORGE GRIFFITH. (With Frontispiece.)
For Liberty. By HUME NISBET. (With Frontispiece.)
A Splendid Sin. By GRANT ALLEN.
A Sweet Sinner. By HUME NISBET.
The Eye of Istar. By W. LE QUEUX.
Devil's Dice. By W. LE QUEUX.
The Wooing of May. By ALAN ST. AUBYN.
The Case of Ailsa Gray. By GEORGE MANVILLE FENN.
In Vallombrosa. By ADELINE SERGEANT.
The Great War in England in 1897. By WILLIAM LE QUEUX. (Illustrated.)
Zoraida. By WILLIAM LE QUEUX. (Illustrated.)
The Romance of Golden Star. By GEO. GRIFFITH. (Illustrated.)
In a Grass Country. By Mrs. LOVETT CAMERON. (With Frontispiece.)
The Girl in the Brown Habit. By Mrs. EDWARD KENNARD. (With Frontispiece.)
Two Cousins and a Castle. By Mrs. LOVETT CAMERON.
The Rebel Chief. By HUME NISBET. (Illustrated by the Author.)
A Desert Bride: a Story of Adventure in India and Persia. By HUME NISBET. (With Illustrations by the Author.)
A Bush Girl's Romance. By HUME NISBET. (With Illustrations by the Author.)
Wedded to Sport. By Mrs. EDWARD KENNARD.
Housekeeping: a Guide to Domestic Management. By Mrs. HUMPHRY ("Madge," of *Truth*).
The Queen's Desire: a Romance of the Indian Mutiny. By HUME NISBET. (With Illustrations by the Author.)
Everybody's Favourite. By JOHN STRANGE WINTER.

Novels at Two Shillings and Sixpence.
In 1 Vol., Cloth, Price 2s. 6d. each.

The Truth-Tellers. By JOHN STRANGE WINTER.
The Mystery of Dudley Horne. By FLORENCE WARDEN.
Mrs. Crichton's Creditors. By Mrs. ALEXANDER.
Only a Flirt. By Mrs. JOCELYN.
Into an Unknown World. By JOHN STRANGE WINTER.
The Way of a Woman. By L. T. MEADE.
The Girls at the Grange. By FLORENCE WARDEN.
A Magnificent Young Man. By JOHN STRANGE WINTER.
A Blameless Woman. By the same Author.
A Born Soldier. By the same Author.

14, BEDFORD STREET, STRAND, W.C.

The Soul of the Bishop. By JOHN STRANGE WINTER.
A Seventh Child. By the same Author.
Aunt Johnnie. By the same Author.
The Other Man's Wife. By the same Author.
Beautiful Jim. By the same Author.
Garrison Gossip. By the same Author.
My Geoff. By the same Author. | Only Human. By the same Author.
Mrs. Bob. By the same Author. | A Siege Baby. By the same Author.
The Strange Story of My Life. By the same Author.
The Coming of Chloe. By Mrs. HUNGERFORD.
As it Was in the Beginning. By GEO. R. SIMS.
The Coachman's Club. By the same Author.
Dr. Darch's Wife. By FLORENCE WARDEN.
A Spoilt Girl. By the same Author.
A Man of To-Day. By HELEN MATHERS.
The Man with a Secret. By FERGUS HUME.
Basil and Annette. By B. L. FARJEON.
The March of Fate. By the same Author.
A Young Girl's Life. By the same Author.
Toilers of Babylon. By the same Author.
The Catch of the County. By Mrs. EDWARD KENNARD.
At the Tail of the Hounds. By the same Author.
Fooled by a Woman. By the same Author.
The Plaything of an Hour, and other Stories. By the same Author.
That Pretty Little Horse-Breaker. By the same Author.
The Hunting Girl. By the same Author.
Our Friends in the Hunting Field. By the same Author.
Straight as a Die. By the same Author.
A Riverside Romance. By the same Author.
Matron or Maid? By the same Author.
Just Like a Woman. By the same Author.
Sporting Tales. By the same Author.
Twilight Tales. By the same Author. (Illustrated.)
A Homburg Beauty. By the same Author.
Landing a Prize. By the same Author.
A Crack County. By the same Author.
Little Lady Lee. By Mrs. LOVETT CAMERON.
A Man's Undoing. By the same Author.
A Soul Astray. By the same Author.
A Daughter's Heart. By the same Author.
Tragic Blunder. By the same Author.
Bachelor's Bridal. By the same Author.
Sister's Sin. By the same Author. | Weak Woman. By the same Author.
A Lost Wife. By the same Author.
A Fight with Fate. By Mrs. ALEXANDER.
A Golden Autumn. By the same Author.
Vignettes. By "RITA." | Joan & Mrs. Carr. By the same Author.
The Countess Pharamond; A Sequel to "Sheba." By the same Author.
The Man in Possession. By the same Author.

14, BEDFORD STREET, STRAND, W.C.

Miss Kate. By "RITA."
The Romance of a Châlet. By Mrs. CAMPBELL-PRAED.
The Freaks of Lady Fortune. By MAY CROMMELIN.
Violet Vyvian, M.F.H. By MAY CROMMELIN and J. MORAY BROWN.
Dream Faces. By The Hon. Mrs. FETHERSTONHAUGH.
Sybil Ross's Marriage. By F. C. PHILIPS and C. J. WILLS.
My Face is My Fortune. By F. C. PHILIPS and PERCY FENDALL.
Margaret Byng. By the same Authors.
A Daughter's Sacrifice. By the same Authors.
A Regular Fraud. By Mrs. ROBERT JOCELYN.
Lady Mary's Experiences. By the same Author.
The Criton Hunt Mystery. By the same Author.
For One Season Only. (A Sporting Novel.) By the same Author.
Only a Horse Dealer. By the same Author.
A Big Stake. By the same Author.
Drawn Blank. By the same Author.
The M.F.H.'s Daughter. By the same Author.
Kitty's Engagement. By FLORENCE WARDEN.
Our Widow. By the same Author.
A Perfect Fool. By the same Author.
Strictly Incog.; being the Record of a Passage through Bohemia. By the same Author.
A Lady in Black. By the same Author.
A Wild Wooing. By the same Author.
My Child and I : A Woman's Story. By the same Author.
A Young Wife's Trial; or Ralph Ryder of Brent. By the same Author.
My Love Noel. By HUME NISBET.
The Great Secret ; A Tale of To-morrow. By the same Author.
The Haunted Station, and other Stories. By the same Author.
To Step Aside is Human. By ALAN ST. AUBYN.
In the Sweet West Country. By the same Author.
Told in the Twilight. By ADELINE SERGEANT.

New Series of Novels at Two Shillings.
In Cloth, Price 2s. each.

A Son of Ishmael. By L. T. MEADE.
A Proctor's Wooing. By ALAN ST. AUBYN.
Cursed by a Fortune. By GEORGE MANVILLE FENN.

NOVELS AT TWO SHILLINGS.

In Picture Boards, Price 2s. each.

A Magnificent Young Man. By JOHN STRANGE WINTER.
The Strange Story of My Life. By the same Author.
A Blameless Woman. By the same Author.
A Born Soldier. By the same Author.
In the Sweet West Country. By ALAN ST. AUBYN.
To Step Aside is Human. By the same Author.
The Great Secret. BY HUME NISBET.
My Love Noel. By the same Author.
A Seventh Child. By JOHN STRANGE WINTER.
The Soul of the Bishop. By the same Author.
Aunt Johnnie. By the same Author. | My Geoff. By the same Author.
Only Human. By the same Author. | Mrs. Bob. By the same Author.
The Other Man's Wife. By the same Author.
Beautiful Jim. By the same Author. | A Siege Baby. By the same Author.
Garrison Gossip. By the same Author.
Army Society: Life in a Garrison Town. By the same Author.
Devil's Dice. By WILLIAM LE QUEUX.
A Fight with Fate. By Mrs. ALEXANDER.
A Golden Autumn. By the same Author.
A Man of To-day. By HELEN MATHERS.
A Splendid Sin. By GRANT ALLEN.
A Man with a Secret. By FERGUS HUME.
Sporting Tales. By Mrs. EDWARD KENNARD.
The Catch of the County. By the same Author.
The Hunting Girl. By the same Author.
Just Like a Woman. By the same Author.
Matron or Maid? By the same Author. | Wedded to Sport. By the same Author.
That Pretty Little Horsebreaker. By the same Author.
A Homburg Beauty. By the same Author.
Our Friends in the Hunting-Field. By the same Author.
Landing a Prize. By the same Author. | A Crack County. By the same Author.
Straight as a Die. By the same Author.
The Plaything of an Hour. By the same Author.
The Sorrows of a Golfer's Wife. By the same Author.

14, BEDFORD STREET, STRAND, W.C.

A Riverside Romance. By Mrs. EDWARD KENNARD.
As it was in the Beginning. By G. R. SIMS.
The Coachman's Club. By the same Author.
A Soul Astray. By Mrs. LOVETT CAMERON.
A Tragic Blunder. By the same Author.
Little Lady Lee. By the same Author.
A Bachelor's Bridal. By the same Author.
A Daughter's Heart. By the same Author.
A Lost Wife. By the same Author. | **Weak Woman.** By the same Author.
A Sister's Sin. By the same Author. | **Jack's Secret.** By the same Author.
The March of Fate. By B. L. FARJEON.
Toilers of Babylon. By the same Author.
Basil and Annette. By the same Author.
A Young Girl's Life. By the same Author.
Strictly Incog. By FLORENCE WARDEN. | **A Perfect Fool.** By the same Author.
My Child and I : A Woman's Story. By the same Author.
Our Widow. By the same Author.
A Woman's Face. By the same Author.
A Young Wife's Trial; or, Ralph Ryder of Brent. By the same Author.
A Wild Wooing. By the same Author. | **Dr. Darch's Wife.** By the same Author.
A Lady in Black. By the same Author. | **A Spoilt Girl.** By the same Author.
Kitty's Engagement. By the same Author.
The Man in Possession. By "RITA." | **Vignettes.** By the same Author.
Joan and Mrs. Carr. By the same Author.
Miss Kate. By the same Author.
A Modern Bridegroom. By Mrs. ALEXANDER FRASER.
The Romance of a Châlet. By Mrs. CAMPBELL-PRAED.
Violet Vyvian, M.F.H. By MAY CROMMELIN and J. MORAY BROWN.
The Freaks of Lady Fortune. By MAY CROMMELIN.
Sybil Ross's Marriage. By F. C. PHILIPS and C. J. WILLS.
My Face is My Fortune. By F. C. PHILIPS and PERCY FENDALL.
A Daughter's Sacrifice. By the same Authors.
A Desert Bride. By HUME NISBET. | **The Rebel Chief.** By the same Author.
A Bush Girl's Romance. By the same Author.
The Queen's Desire. By the same Author.
A Sweet Sinner. By the same Author.
Drawn Blank. By Mrs. ROBERT JOCELYN.
For One Season Only: a Sporting Novel. By the same Author.
The M.F.H.'s Daughter. By the same Author.
Only a Horse-Dealer. By the same Author.
A Big Stake. By the same Author.
The Criton Hunt Mystery. By the same Author.
A Regular Fraud. By the same Author.
The Case of Ailsa Gray. By G. MANVILLE FENN.
A Tragic Honeymoon. By ALAN ST. AUBYN.
The Wooing of May. By the same Author.
Told in the Twilight. By ADELINE SERGEANT.
The Romance of Golden Star. By GEORGE GRIFFITHS.

ONE SHILLING NOVELS.

In Paper Covers. Also in Cloth, 1s. 6d.

Two Husbands. By JOHN STRANGE WINTER.
In the Same Regiment. By the same Author.
A Seaside Flirt. By the same Author.
A Gay Little Woman. By the same Author.
The Troubles of an Unlucky Boy. By the same Author.
Grip. By the same Author.
The Same Thing with a Difference. By the same Author.
I Loved Her Once. By the same Author.
I Married a Wife. By the same Author.
Private Tinker, and Other Stories. By the same Author. (Illustrated.).
The Major's Favourite. By the same Author.
The Stranger Woman. By the same Author.
Red Coats. By the same Author. | A Man's Man. By the same Author.
That Mrs. Smith. By the same Author.
Three Girls. By the same Author. | Mere Luck. By the same Author.
Lumley the Painter. By the same Author.
Good-bye. By the same Author.
He Went for a Soldier. By the same Author.
Ferrers Court. By the same Author. | Buttons. By the same Author.
A Little Fool. By the same Author.
My Poor Dick. By the same Author. (Illustrated by MAURACE GREIFFENHAGEN.)
Bootles' Children. By the same Author. (Illustrated by J. BERNARD PARTRIDGE.)
The Confessions of a Publisher. By the same Author.
Mignon's Husband. By the same Author.
That Imp. By the same Author. | Mignon's Secret. By the same Author.
On March. By the same Author. | In Quarters. By the same Author.
A Madonna of the Music Halls. By W. LE QUEUX.
Dorcas Dene, Detective. By G. R. SIMS.
Dorcas Dene, Detective. (Second Series.) By the same Author.
The Courage of Pauline. By MORLEY ROBERTS.
A Woman with a History. By WEEDON GROSSMITH.
A Devil in Nun's Veiling. By F. C. PHILIPS.
The Luckiest of Three. By the same Author.
The Investigations of John Pym. By DAVID CHRISTIE MURRAY.
The Power of an Eye. By Mrs. FRANK ST. CLAIR GRIMWOOD.
The Gentleman Who Vanished. By FERGUS HUME.
Miss Mephistopheles. By the same Author.
The Man Who Didn't. By Mrs. LOVETT CAMERON.
In a Grass Country; a Story of Love and Sport. By the same Author.
The Confessions of a Door-mat. By ALFRED C. CALMOUR.
The Mystery of a Woman's Heart. By Mrs. EDWARD KENNARD.
A Guide Book for Lady Cyclists. By the same Author.
The Woman with the Diamonds. By FLORENCE WARDEN.
Two Lads and a Lass. By the same Author.
City and Suburban. By the same Author.
A Scarborough Romance. By the same Author.
Continental Chit Chat. By MABEL HUMBERT.
Piscatorial Patches. By MARTIN PESCADOR.
The Blue Diamonds: A Tale of Ceylon. By LELIA BOUSTEAD.
A Near Thing. By H. CUMBERLAND BENTLEY.

F. V. WHITE & CO., PUBLISHERS 15

The Welcome Library.

(With which is incorporated "THE MODERN NOVELIST.")

A NEW MONTHLY SERIES OF FICTION . . .
. . . . BY POPULAR AUTHORS.

In Paper Covers, 3d. each.

By DORA RUSSELL.
1. FOR THE CHILD'S SAKE.
By MRS. HUNGERFORD.
2. A CONQUERING HEROINE.
By MRS. ALEXANDER FRASER.
3. SHE CAME BETWEEN.
By LADY CONSTANCE HOWARD.
4. SWEETHEART AND WIFE.
By FLORENCE MARRYAT.
5. FOR A WOMAN'S PLEASURE.
By F. C. PHILIPS.
6. EXTENUATING CIRCUMSTANCES.
By JEAN MIDDLEMASS.
7. ALL FOR LOVE.
By ANNIE THOMAS.
8. THE OLD LOVE AGAIN.
By MRS. HUNGERFORD.
9. HER LAST THROW.
By FLORENCE MARRYAT.
10. A LUCKY DISAPPOINTMENT.
By THEO GIFT.
11. LADY BETTY'S CHANCES.
By JEAN MIDDLEMASS.
12. LOVE'S SPOILED DARLING.
By MRS. ALEXANDER.
13. A FALSE SCENT.
By ANNIE THOMAS.
14. VICTOR'S WIDOW.
By THEO GIFT.
15. AN UGLY SECRET.

By JEAN MIDDLEMASS.
16. HER LOVE AND HIS LIFE.
By MRS. LEITH ADAMS.
17. MABEL MEREDITH'S LOVE STORY.
By ANNIE THOMAS.
18. A GOOD SETTLEMENT.
By THEO GIFT.
19. A YOUNG MAN AND HIS FOLLY.
By MRS. LEITH ADAMS.
20. LADY DEANE.
By FLORENCE MARRYAT.
21. SIR MARCUS'S CHOICE.
By F. C. PHILIPS.
22. A FRENCH MARRIAGE.
By MRS. LEITH ADAMS.
23. CICELY DENNISON.
By F. C. PHILIPS.
24. A DEVIL IN NUN'S VEILING.
By MRS. LEITH ADAMS.
25. LOTTIE.
By OLIVE MOLESWORTH.
26. MR. ROBINSON.
By MRS. LOVETT CAMERON.
27. THE MADNESS OF MARRIAGE.
By MRS. DE COURCY LAFFAN.
28. GEORGIE'S WOOER.
By F. C. PHILIPS.
29. JACK AND THREE JILLS.

OTHERS TO FOLLOW.

14, BEDFORD STREET, STRAND, W.C.

MISCELLANEOUS SERIES.

GOOD FORM:
A Book of Every-Day Etiquette.
By MRS. ARMSTRONG,
Author of "MODERN ETIQUETTE IN PUBLIC AND PRIVATE."

Limp Cloth, 2s.

LETTERS TO A BRIDE,
Including Letters to a Débutante.
By MRS. ARMSTRONG.

Cloth Gilt, 2s. 6d.

HOUSEKEEPING:
A Guide to Domestic Management.
By MRS. HUMPHRY ("Madge," of "Truth").

Revised Edition, Cloth, 3s. 6d.

TURF CELEBRITIES I HAVE KNOWN.
By WILLIAM DAY,
AUTHOR OF
"THE RACEHORSE IN TRAINING,"
"REMINISCENCES OF THE TURF," &c.
. . . WITH A PORTRAIT OF THE AUTHOR . . .

1 Vol., Gilt Cloth, 16s.

14, BEDFORD STREET, STRAND, W.C.

www.ingramcontent.com/pod-product-compliance
Lightning Source LLC
Chambersburg PA
CBHW020755230426
43666CB00007B/708